Advance Praise for
The End of the World As We Know It

"Chuck Smith, jr's wonderful and well-written book will introduce you to postmodernity and its challenges and opportunities for Christian life and action. But it will do far more. It will also open up for you a new and more productive way of relating to our changing culture: not withdrawing to a Christian ghetto, not critiquing from a distance, not assimilating to lose our distinctiveness, but rather engaging our culture, understanding it, penetrating it, and with God's help, transforming it."

> —BRIAN MCLAREN
>
> pastor of Cedar Ridge Community Church in Maryland
> and author of *The Church on the Other Side* and *Finding Faith*

"The most user-friendly and useful introduction to ministry in postmodern culture yet written. After this book, no leader, no church can keep playing the 'conscientious objector from postmodernism' game."

> —LEONARD SWEET
>
> Drew University professor and author of the postmodern evangelism
> trilogy *SoulTsunami, AquaChurch,* and *SoulSalsa*

"Chuck Smith, jr. offers an accessible guide to the new postmodern world that is rapidly replacing the old modern world. He voices a needed call for a robust, positive Christian engagement with the 'pop culture' that has become the central expression of the emerging postmodern ethos. He offers sound advice on how Christians can truly be pioneers and explorers as a gospel people in the postmodern context."

> —STANLEY J. GRENZ
>
> Pioneer McDonald Professor of Theology and Ethics
> Carey/Regent College, Vancouver BC, Canada
> and author of *A Primer on Postmodernism*

"Of all the books I have read on postmodernity, this one is unquestionably the most understandable and the most useful. This book is as much an excellent worldview as it is an urgent and necessary call to have one. A must-read for people who want to communicate to their generation or simply understand their own kids (or their parents, for that matter)."

—JOHN FISCHER

author of *12 Steps for the Recovering Pharisee (like me)*

"Chuck Smith, jr. has a rare gift of not only engaging the complex culture of postmodernity but of being able to interpret it in a most helpful way for other pastors and lay leaders. He writes both as a pastor and a parent who has had to wrestle with the issues and his own emotional responses. This is not a book about postmodernity but one that immerses the reader in postmodernity with a fund of stories and illustrations and perceptive analysis and evaluation. He also helps us to see how the Word of God addresses this complex cultural context."

—EDDIE GIBBS

Donald A. McGavran Professor, Church Growth School
of World Mission, Fuller Seminary, Pasadena, California

THE END
OF THE
WORLD
...AS WE
KNOW IT

CLEAR DIRECTION FOR BOLD AND INNOVATIVE
MINISTRY IN A POSTMODERN WORLD

THE END OF THE WORLD ... AS WE KNOW IT

CHUCK SMITH, JR.

WATERBROOK
PRESS

THE END OF THE WORLD...AS WE KNOW IT
PUBLISHED BY WATERBROOK PRESS
2375 Telstar Drive, Suite 160
Colorado Springs, Colorado 80920
A division of Random House, Inc.

ISBN 1-57856-402-6

Published in association with Sealy M. Yates, Literary Agent, Orange, California.

Library of Congress Cataloging-in-Publication Data
Smith, Chuck, 1951–
    The end of the world, as we know it : clear direction for bold and innovative ministry in
a postmodern world / Chuck Smith, Jr.—1st ed.
       p. cm.
   ISBN 1-57856-402-6
    1. Postmodernism—Religious aspects—Christianity. 2. Church work. I. Title.

BR115.P74 S65 2001
261—dc21

                                                                00-049788

Printed in the United States of America
2001—First Edition

10 9 8 7 6 5 4 3 2 1

Contents

Acknowledgments ix

Preface: *Learn from My Mistake* xi

Introduction: *A New World in Disguise* 1

1. *Culture-Quake* 11

2. *The Unraveling of Modernity* 27

3. *Getting a Handle on Postmodernity* 45

4. *Postmodernism and Popular Culture* 63

5. *Postmodern Faith* 89

6. *The Church and the Postmodern Bazaar* 115

7. *Online with Gen X* 143

8. *Storytellers and Soul Healers* 171

Notes 199

100377

Acknowledgments

There are many people who deserve my gratitude for making this book possible, yet deserve none of the blame for its shortcomings. Many thanks to my friend and "pastoral researcher," John Hallowell, who several years ago introduced me to postmodernism. Thanks to Dan Rich and the other kind people at WaterBrook Press who have given me invaluable assistance. Thanks to Ron Lee for his editing suggestions, encouragement, and keen eye. Thanks to Lela Gilbert for believing in me and for prodding me along. Thanks to Chuck Fromm for always being there. Thanks to Craig Whittaker, the rest of my church staff, and our whole congregation for being so courageously supportive. Thanks to my five children—Will, Jenn, Mike, Kare, and Scott—for their loving sacrifices. Thanks to Mom and Dad for everything. Thanks to my wife, Barbara, whose help and love have made this dream, and many others, come true. And, of course, my greatest thanks to God.

LEARN FROM
MY MISTAKE

I am a child of the sixties. But not really.

Demographically I belong to the baby-boom generation, and therefore I should have been a child of the sixties. But though I lived through that infamous decade, I was not a participant. I cannot even say I was a spectator because from an early age I had been taught to turn my eyes away from the "world."

My religious heritage effectively cut me out of the dominant culture of North America during my adolescence. Because I belonged to a fundamentalist subculture, I was isolated from the culture of my peers. The moral values of my religious subculture, for the most part, consisted of negatives: We did not smoke, did not go to dances, did not play cards, did not go to movies, did not "party," did not go to rock concerts, did not join in political rallies, and so on. These prohibitions may have been exaggerated in my case because I was a pastor's kid.

Problems arose for me because even though I looked exactly like everyone else in my age group, I lived worlds apart. Based only on external appearance, there would have been no way to discern that the difference between me and my peers was as great as that between a Boy Scout and a Martian. Not only did I feel alienated from others, I also internalized that alienation and concluded that I was "weird," somehow inherently flawed. On the outside I looked like everyone else. On the inside I was different.

There is no one to blame for my cultural and psychological dissonance because it resulted from truly good people doing what they thought to be right. And I am not alone. Thousands of children from fundamentalist homes shared my experience of being strangers to their own generation. Unfortunately, many from my religious subculture abandoned their faith. Their reasoning went something like this: If I am going to hell because I smoked a cigarette, then I might as well indulge in every vice.

Since that time I have discovered Mansell Pattison's neat explanation of this predicament. The "fundamentalist value system," in his words, was once "the dominant value system of America. However, since the closing of the frontier, the industrialization and urbanization of America, this value system has become obsolescent." For example, by the sixties there were many card games that did not entail whiskey, gambling, cigars, or barroom brawls. The ban on playing cards did not have the same significance that it did one hundred years earlier.

Fundamentalists could have reexamined their interpretations of Scripture in the light of cultural change, but instead they insisted that their interpretations were as fixed and infallible as the Bible itself. So, in Pattison's words, they have "clung to their value system in the face of increasing social and psychological dissonance. The price they have paid is measured in terms of personal and social dysfunction in participation in the society as a whole." This was my profile exactly.

This explains why, in spite of the exciting and world-changing aspects of the sixties, I passed through them in a kind of catatonic stupor. It was a great time to be alive—for those who were alive. I envied my "worldly" Presbyterian friends who did not seem to struggle with guilt as I did and who enjoyed more participation in mainstream culture. My own experience of the sixties era was held in a kind of suspended animation until the decade was almost over.

Eventually, though, I recognized how outdated, parochial, and rigid the fundamentalist subculture had become. This awakening came when pioneering Christian rocker Larry Norman retrieved a war cry of Martin Luther: "Why does the devil have all the good music?" The question scandalized my generation of fundamentalists. We didn't doubt that the prince of darkness cornered the market on all the good music and the reason was obvious: "The 'good music' was rock-'n'-roll."

Norman maintained that the church should make use of the best contemporary music to communicate the truth of Christ to a new generation. Even though I agreed with him, I came late to the party. I had already missed my own era. I do not regret the fact that I never got stoned, never contracted an STD, never lived on the streets, and never freaked out on acid. But there were many legitimate events, trends, and social gatherings that I avoided as well. And being so radically isolated from my culture stunted my intellectual, social, and psychological development. Furthermore, I was neither salt nor light to my peers. Whatever witness I could have had I botched through irrelevance, my deep-rooted insecurity, and my occasional outbursts of judgmental condemnation of my classmates.

Have we learned anything since the sixties? A Christian culture forms within a larger host culture and exercises a certain kind of influence. But as time goes on, the host culture mutates. Old institutions collapse, new structures emerge, and people who cling to the past face a crisis of irrelevance. Christians who withdraw from their host culture forfeit their effectiveness in influencing and changing it.

I have written this book because we have come to a crucial moment in history. We are undergoing one of the most radical cultural transformations of the last three or four centuries, and there is a very real danger that

Christians will again find themselves on the sidelines, helplessly watching the world transform. If the church is determined to do no more than preserve the past, we will lose the future. But if we seize the future that is already upon us, we stand a good chance of reinserting Christian faith into the life of our dominant culture to a degree that has been unknown in the last two hundred years.

If you choose to adopt this second option, then you had better get a helmet.

CHURCH
―――――――――――――
DOMINANT CULTURE / HOST CULTURE

THE END

OF THE

WORLD

...AS WE

KNOW IT

A NEW WORLD
IN DISGUISE

Eddie leaned forward, resting his arms on the table. His eyes were dark and troubled. The restaurant with an outdoor patio was my idea, as I anticipated another sunny day in Southern California. Fishing boats tied up at the nearby docks rocked gently in the water. They would rise occasionally on the ripple created by a passing vessel, and their lines would squeak on the dock cleats. Seagulls flew close by, and a few pelicans floated in the water at the far side of the harbor. All in all it was a peaceful afternoon. The expression on Eddie's face, however, was anything but peaceful.

Eddie is a close friend whose life temporarily had moved out of my orbit. When we bumped into each other one day, I realized how much I had missed his irrepressible humor, winsome grin, and sharp mind. We exchanged e-mail addresses and promised to keep in touch. In his second e-mail to me I sensed a note of desperation, so we made plans to meet for lunch at the marina. As the warm sunlight found our bald spots, we spent a few minutes talking about our lives since our last meeting. Then Eddie got serious, and the words tumbled out.

"Does it seem to you that everything in the world is going crazy? For example, I tried really hard to raise my sons to be independent, to work hard, to care about others. But my oldest son, whose marriage is falling apart, just moved back home with a ton of debt, no job, and hardly an ounce of ambition. I sure don't get what's going on.

"Everyone is convinced they're entitled to wealth without work, sacrifice, or saving. Instead they look for their first opportunity to sue somebody. That's their financial plan: Sue somebody. And why do so many people have an addiction to shopping? What happened to the simple pleasures? And what about all the violence in the streets and the schools? Doesn't that ever get to you?"

"Stop," I said. "You're depressing me!"

But he continued on with the list of things that were bothering him, from bizarre stories in the newspapers to his despair over whether he could even trust newspapers. After a few minutes he seemed to run out of steam. Actually he was only catching his breath. Then he brought up the big question. "And how do you think God feels about all of this? He can't like it, so why doesn't He do something? Do you ever wonder if maybe He doesn't do anything because He's simply not there?"

It was obvious Eddie had given a lot of thought to society, politics, education, family, religion, money, and all the other stuff that fills our everyday lives. He was confused, frustrated, and deeply troubled. In fact, he was having difficulty sleeping at night because his world seemed to be tumbling—throwing everything out of place. He also found that his usual laugh-your-way-out-of-trouble approach was not working.

Because Eddie trusted my insight and our friendship, his questions were sincere; he genuinely wanted my help in explaining why the world seems so *weird.* He also wanted reassurance that it was still reasonable to believe that God had His hand on society and that somehow His will would be done on earth as it is in heaven.

The world in which Eddie and I grew up is disappearing, and though the new world replacing it might look the same, it is actually very different. My friend was experiencing symptoms of *displacement*—when you think you belong somewhere, but that "somewhere" is no longer your home. (It's like when John Cusack returns to his childhood home in *Grosse Pointe Blank* only to discover a convenience store standing in its place.) Eddie missed the good old days when right was right and wrong was wrong.

The simple, common-sense logic that used to give life meaning no longer works. The basic structures of society have become complex and vague. It is easy to blame our feeling of dissonance on the sinfulness of our culture. But that tends to oversimplify, and therefore ignore, the radical changes that have taken place. Rather than confronting these changes, too often the Christian sighs deeply and says, "I sure hope Jesus comes back soon!"

But Eddie wasn't the type to stick his head in the sand. He wanted some answers. While trying to help him understand what he was feeling, I asked if he had heard the word *postmodernism.* He thought he had seen it somewhere but had no idea what it meant. As I began to explain my own thoughts about postmodernism, it was like a light turned on for him. He was beginning to learn a new way to make sense of a changed world.

Classroom Confusion

It's not just dads like Eddie who are trying to find their way in a postmodern world. The influence of postmodernism has filtered down to school classrooms. That's where Brandon, who was struggling with high-school English, experienced the confusion that postmodernism can produce. Brandon's trouble in English class was not due to poor study habits, but to the way the subject was being taught.

"You would think that the author of a story would have something to do with the meaning of the story!" Brandon complained to his mother. "Our assignment was to read *Anna Karenina* and be prepared to discuss it in class. Reading through it, I thought the author must have been a Christian, which would help explain what he was trying to do in the plot. But my teacher said the author wasn't important. Instead she wanted us to give our own impressions of what we felt the story meant. So instead of studying the story, all we've been doing is reading it and keeping a journal of our impressions and ideas, which we share with the rest of the class. I don't think my teacher wants us to look for the author's meaning."

Brandon was right. His teacher was not concerned with the author's intent because many teachers believe if authors speak for themselves—especially dead, white, male authors—their "message" reinforces the imbalance of power in society: the strong over the weak, the rich over the poor, males over females, and so on. But, they believe, if students are allowed to determine the meaning of a book (or "text") without regard for the author's intent, then they share the *author*-ity, which may lead to a greater balance of power. The power of interpretation is thus given to readers, and no view is regarded as superior or inferior to another, with one possible exception: Many teachers have a bias against Christian points of view.

When Christian parents ask, "What are our children learning in school?" they are rightfully concerned. Are the Christian values taught at home reinforced at school, or undermined? Are students learning information and skills that will prepare them to live productive, wholesome, and generous lives as adults? Or are they learning random facts in a context where the same senseless worldview is promoted that one sees on television and in motion pictures? Who eliminated the "authors" of books?[1] How did they pull off that feat and on what grounds? Again, the word *postmodernism* arises as an answer.

Trial by Story

America's legal system is undergoing a transformation just as significant as the changes we see in public education. A new breed of legal scholars is pushing for an approach to law in which court cases are argued on the basis of compelling stories rather than legal reasoning. These scholars believe that the logical process of analyzing the facts of a case favors certain types of people and prejudices judges and juries against others. Instead of the traditional approach to law, they argue, judges and juries should be won over with heart-touching stories, stories with emotional impact that can produce the outcome desired by the lawyers.

Law professors Suzanna Sherry and Daniel Farber ran across this movement while reading law-review articles. In response to what they read, Sherry explained in an interview with Ken Meyers,[2] she and Farber "wrote an article that we thought was actually quite friendly to the storytelling movement. We said, 'There's a place for this and we think it's a great development, but perhaps there ought to be some safeguards.' For example, the stories ought to be typical and truthful and somehow tied to legal analysis."

That balanced response drew a firestorm of criticism from the advocates of storytelling in the courtroom. "You've got us all wrong," they cried. They were not interested in objective truth but in the power of a good story in winning verdicts for their clients. After all, if legal reasoning alone were applied to the case, their clients might be put at a disadvantage. At that point, Suzanna Sherry says, she "realized that it was more than just a movement, a type of scholarship; it was a whole different worldview."

"Their policy recommendations are always whatever is good for my particular group...," she continued. "Human beings don't really reason, they think emotionally, they think in terms of mind-sets, that is, particular views of reality. What the radicals suggest is that because the white-male power establishment has been in charge of constructing reality, that all of our current mind-sets are what white males want us to think, and that the only way to destroy those mind-sets—to replace them with other mind-sets—is to tell these sorts of stories that are emotional, that tug at the heartstrings, and so on."

It's no wonder that every year more Americans have to purchase liability insurance to protect themselves from lawsuits. When we hear of people—even criminals—being awarded compensation for injuries sustained while trespassing on another person's property, we cannot help but wonder what has happened to the ideals of justice and truth.

According to Sherry, the stories told in court cases tend to be about victimization. "And it is the person with the greatest claim to victimhood or the greatest pain whose story is heard." Where did this idea come from, that *storytelling* is the way to establish a legal precedent, win an argument, or champion a cause? Once again, the answer lies in the word *postmodernism*.

Political Failure

Just as postmodernism is transforming the legal system, public education, and the broader culture, it also is turning the political system upside-down. Efforts by conservative Christians to become engaged in politics and push for policies that reflect biblical values have largely failed, at least in the view of some who helped create the Religious Right.

Ed Dobson, a former member of the Moral Majority's board of directors, eventually came to question whether biblical goals can be achieved through political means. "During the height of the Moral Majority, we were taking in millions of dollars a year," he said. "We published a magazine, organized state chapters, lobbied Congress, aired a radio program, and more. Did it work? Is the moral condition of America better because of our efforts? Even a casual observation of the current moral climate suggests that despite all the time, money, and energy—despite the political power—we failed. Things have not gotten better; they have gotten worse."[3]

For a brief spell, Christians who identified with the Religious Right were caught up in the heady exhilaration of political clout. Once given credit for the political victories of Jimmy Carter and Ronald Reagan, they came to believe nothing could stop them from bringing America "back to its Christian roots." However, national events within the last few years have disheartened some of the movement's staunchest supporters. Cal Thomas, former vice president of communications for the Moral Majority, said, "Two decades after conservative Christians charged into the political arena, bringing new voters and millions of dollars with them in hopes of transforming the culture through political power, it must now be acknowledged that we have failed."[4]

Perhaps we are just beginning to realize the consequences of Francis Schaefer's observation that the United States is a "post-Christian" nation. Paul Weyrich, who along with Howard Phillips and Jerry Falwell conceived the idea of the Moral Majority, published an open letter in which he commended Christians who still wanted to pursue political reform. But in the same letter he conceded that "the efforts to return some semblance of moral order to the nation through the political process have failed."[5] He perceived in President Bill Clinton's ability to stay in office—despite the Justice Department's investigation and his impeachment and trial by Congress—as evidence "that the advocates of morality have lost, and lost badly. This is just the beginning." In Weyrich's view, Christians now find themselves on the defensive against a hostile government and culture.

Given the demise of the Religious Right, what new tactic should conservative Christians adopt? According to Weyrich, "We are now going to have to examine parallel institutions with which we can win the culture war"—institutions such as home schooling and alternative radio, for example. Weyrich believes that Christians must shift to a new battlefield outside mainstream culture if they are to preserve their values and eventually influence the wider culture. (Later we will see why the term "culture war" is a misleading, ineffective, and unbiblical metaphor for Christian presence and witness in the world.)

The Meaning of Postmodernism

What has happened in American society and politics in the last twenty years to dash the dreams of such sturdy advocates of Christian political activism? What has happened to the soul of our nation—to its commitment to truth, values, and decency?

Consider this insight from Lynne Cheney, who formerly chaired the National Endowment for the Humanities. "People who have not been in college in the last ten years or so are unlikely to understand how discredited ideas like truth and objectivity have become."[6] It is not only truth that suffers but every discipline and belief derived from the notion of truth. "In fields ranging from education to art to law, the attack on truth has been accompanied by an assault on standards. The connection is seldom made clear." The streams of thought that have undermined truth and standards, according to Cheney, flow from a source called postmodernism.

The term *postmodernism* is not easy to define because it is not one, complete, coherent movement or system of thought. A variety of definitions can be found in different fields of research, and some people claim it defies definition altogether.[7] To further complicate matters, some of the historians, philosophers, and writers who have been most influential in articulating postmodern themes refuse to be called postmodern.

So how does the word *postmodern* explain Eddie's sense of confusion with today's world? Brandon's frustration over the disregard of the author in literary analysis? Suzanna Sherry's discovery that "truth" is less important than a compelling story when arguing a legal case? And the decision by former leaders of the Religious Right to abandon politics?

As this book addresses these questions, I hope to provide you with a good understanding of where our society is going and how Christians can play a significant role in our changing culture. Do not misunderstand: The future will not be easy. I am afraid many believers will retreat from the hard work that lies ahead. But those who hesitate will miss out on a great work of God that is now taking shape.

The changes in our society are going to create new opportunities for Christians to influence their communities and expand God's work in the world. We have not seen such a crucial period in church history for at least two hundred years, and how we respond may affect the church for the next two hundred years. We may have to discard some of our old wineskins, but whatever lies ahead, God is already out there, and He has invited us to follow.

If you have surrendered your life to Jesus Christ as both your Lord and Savior, then you have good reason to be confident regarding your role in God's work during the next period of history. Like the virtuous woman of Proverbs 31, you will be able to "laugh at the days to come" (verse 25), but you will need a road map to find your way around in this new terrain. It is my hope that this book will provide that map.

Chapter 1

CULTURE-QUAKE

"When the foundations are being destroyed,
what can the righteous do?"
The LORD is in his holy temple;
the LORD is on his heavenly throne.

PSALM 11:3-4

When my son Will was in the sixth grade, I helped him one night with his science homework. He was studying plate tectonics. We learned that the earth's surface is affected by the actions of huge underground plates on which it rests, and these plates sometimes shift.

There are three types of "plate boundaries," the borders where plates meet: spreading zones (where the plates are moving apart), fracture zones (where plates slide past each other), and converging zones (where plates collide). The movements of these mammoth subterranean plates cause earthquakes on the planet's surface. Living in California, and not too far from the quake-prone San Andreas fault, we found this information fascinating.

There's a cultural parallel to plate tectonics. Underneath the surface of our daily lives, tremendous movement has been taking place—shifts in thinking and in what philosophers call our worldview. The rapid pace of innovation, communication, and change has caused a "cultural earthquake," radiating tremors of confusion into every corner of society. As social

11

analyst Daniel Yankelovich has said: "Increasingly in recent years, our studies of the public show the 'giant plates' of American culture shifting relentlessly beneath us. The shifts create huge dislocations in our lives. Those living closest to society's fault lines are the first to be thrown into new predicaments. But even those living at a remote distance feel the tremors."[1]

We are living on a cultural fault line between two epochal periods. Under our lives huge sociological plates have met and created the disturbances we have felt in our everyday lives and culture. These two periods are the modern era and the postmodern era, and we are living in the transitional stage as the former gives way to the latter.

What do all these shifts mean? Are they good or bad? And what happens to the life we had built on the old landscape? Or, as David asks in Psalm 11, "When the foundations are being destroyed, what can the righteous do?" (verse 3).

By "the righteous," David the poet-king means people who are trying to live right lives—right with God, with others, and with themselves. What should these people do if the beliefs and values on which they have built their lives are disintegrating? What course should they take if the very quest for "rightness" is being abandoned as a hopeless waste of time? One way to begin answering these questions is to take a look at our changing culture.

Culture Shock

Normally, our culture is invisible to us, hiding in the backdrop of our lives—much like water is to fish. We live and move around within culture without being aware of its presence and influence, and reflect on it only when we are introduced to another culture very different from our own. That is when we encounter culture shock.

A variation of culture shock is future shock, which Alvin Toffler described in a 1971 book by the same name. He defined future shock "as the disorientation and stress brought on by trying to cope with too many changes in too short a time."[2] This acceleration of events and reaction times so alters the cultural landscape that it no longer looks like our culture, but like something entirely different.

The future shock we face today is intensified. That is due not only to the amount of change and how rapidly it is occurring, but also to the nature of the change itself. We are witnessing a magnitude of change that is *altering reality*, and that is the real dynamism behind our sense of shock. The question we face is not how quickly is the future coming but how different is our immediate future from our recent past and our present? We are shocked by the weirdness of our own culture. Consider this pop culture message:

"There are no genders."

"There is no age."

"There are no infirmities."

"There are only minds."

We might wish this were a biblical promise of some future Golden Age. But it's not. These statements appeared in an ad for Internet access through MCI. The commercial continues: *"Utopia? No. (No.) The Internet, where minds, doors and lives open up. Is this a great time or what?:)"*

The linking of computers, along with the aggressive development of software programs for sending video streams as well as still images and text, has created the world of cyberspace. In that nowhere, yet everywhere geography between computers, one can remain anonymous, either as a voyeur of other people's Web sites or by creating a cyberidentity that makes it impossible for others to know anything about one's true identity. This cyberworld did not even exist when I was a teenager, yet some people spend almost as much time in it—even earning their livelihood through it—as they do the real world. What can we say about a world where the words *virtual* and *reality* can be used together to describe an environment detached from physical space? Today's reality is different, and that is shocking![3]

Culture-Quake Victims

There is a psychological price to pay for living in a period of transition and social upheaval. Just as astronauts have to cope with weightlessness while traveling in space, so we have to cope with the disorientation we experience while traveling through the space between the modern and postmodern eras. This condition is much more serious than the uneasiness and insecurity some adults feel when introduced to advances in technology. "Panic attack" is closer to the mark.

When the phrase *generation gap* first appeared, it referred to the difficulty in communication between adults and their children. It could have been a gap of twenty to forty years. Nowadays, because of the speed-up of our lives, we can almost define a generation gap as the psychological distance between graduating high school seniors and incoming freshmen. Douglas Coupland (playfully?) invented the term "historical overdosing" in the margin of his book *Generation X* and defined it as living "in a period where too much seems to happen. Major symptoms include addiction to newspapers, magazines, and TV news broadcasts."[4] Our world is doing cartwheels, so we run to the television because we need help in making sense of all the information we receive, to get our bearings, and to find our identity. We are not only overdosing on history; we are in historical transition. Traveling in the space between these eras affects us in a number of uncomfortable ways.

One of those effects is *disorientation*. Imagine waking up one morning in a *Twilight Zone* in which every traffic sign meant something different from the day before. Imagine cars in one lane stopping at intersections for blue lights and in the next lane proceeding on flashing white lights. What if all the traffic signs you are accustomed to reading suddenly had different meanings? You would have a hard time safely crossing a street. That is the magnitude of the current changes in our world.

A few years ago my children and I enjoyed a trip to Australia for a Christian conference. While we were there, a family loaned us their van so we could take in some of the sights. Because Australians drive on the left, it took me awhile to get used to driving on the "wrong" side of the road and shifting gears with my left hand. My oldest son, Will, amused himself counting the number of times I misjudged my distance to the curb and ran over it while turning.

When you have lived for a while in one culture, you become familiar not only with its posted rules but also its unwritten and invisible rules. You are trained to act appropriately in every situation. However, as soon as you step into a foreign culture, the rules change. That is what is happening in our world: The rules are changing. During this time of cultural shift, we are becoming foreigners in our own land.

Another uncomfortable effect of a culture-quake is *ineffectiveness*. Large companies are beginning to discover their methods of management are no longer working. Politicians have found that the rules for running for public office have changed. Christian institutions, too, are beginning to realize that their methods of evangelism, discipleship, and fund-raising simply do not work well anymore. When you always have performed a task in a particular way and have been effective, finding that your efforts and training are no longer useful can leave you immobilized, floundering, and overstocked with lots of answers to questions no one is asking.

A minister friend of mine was speaking at an evangelistic crusade in Chile. He spoke from a platform in the middle of a crowded soccer stadium. At one point a small group of Communist agitators began to whistle and shout slogans in order to disrupt the meeting. My friend asked them several times to be quiet. Then, putting his index finger to his mouth, he blew through his lips, making a "shush" sound. As soon as he did this, a riot broke out, and he had to be escorted away by armed guards. Little did he know that he had just insulted the audience with an obscene gesture. What would have been effective in one cultural setting completely backfired in this setting. In the same way, methods that may have worked powerfully in modernity may prove impotent in postmodernity.

Still another unsettling effect is a *loss of identity*. Personal identity is formed by internal factors as well as by our relationship to our environment. A great many people living today formed their identities in the context of old institutions that are now radically changing or disappearing altogether. As a result we have witnessed the rise of a new pastime involving identity transformation, sometimes referred to as reinventing one's self.

Not only are the old institutions of modernity facing potential obsolescence, but the belief systems that maintained them also are wobbling in the face of postmodern challenges. According to one social analyst, "The collapse of a belief system can be like the end of the world. It can bring down not only the powerful, but whole systems of social roles and the concepts of personal identity that go with them. Even those who are most oppressed by a belief system often fear the loss of it. People can literally cease to know who they are."[5]

The Roots of Modernity

Ours is not the first generation to be thrown off its feet by a culture-quake of such magnitude. The transition from the premodern age to the modern era tossed people into a similar state of chaos. The Industrial Revolution of the late 1700s and 1800s, which became the trademark of the transition into the modern era, forced people to deal with increased knowledge, a changing worldview, and advances in technologies—especially as those technologies affected communication, transportation, and work. In the upheaval, worldviews and ideologies collided, and wars and revolutions erupted between nations, as well as along all levels of society. These birth pangs of the modern age changed forever the way humans regarded life on this planet.[6]

Since we are experiencing a similar culture-quake today, it is important to revisit the roots of modernity to understand its influence in Western society and why it is now disintegrating. Modernity's break with premodernity came in revolutionary stages, the most notable being the Renaissance, the Reformation, and the Enlightenment.

The Renaissance. This is a French word meaning "rebirth" that is used to describe any cultural revival but especially refers to a phenomenon that occurred in Europe from about the 1300s to the 1500s. At the same time that the Roman Catholic Church began to lose its political and cultural dominance, a rediscovery of Greek and Roman art and literature led to a cultural rebirth. Explorers and inventors proliferated during this time—the "Renaissance man," Leonardo da Vinci, comes to mind. As feudal systems began to give way to nation states, economic and political changes spread across Europe. At the heart of the Renaissance was a new conception of human freedom, and the universe shifted from being God-centered to human-centered.

The Reformation. An attempt to reform corruption and abuses within the Roman Catholic Church led instead to the birth of Protestantism. Coming into full flower in the late Renaissance period, the Reformation mirrored in the church the revival going on in secular culture. The Renaissance revisited Greece and Rome for inspiration, whereas the reformers revisited primitive Christianity in the New Testament and early church fathers. Like the secular Renaissance, the Reformation also was influenced by the elevation of humanity in emphasizing the authority of Scripture rather than the church and in stressing the importance of the individual's salvation.

The Enlightenment. Giving birth to the Age of Reason, the Enlightenment was a seventeenth- and eighteenth-century intellectual movement that celebrated human reason over vestiges of medieval superstition. Enlighten-ment thinkers arrived at truth through reason and the five senses, rejecting religion as a source of truth.[7] At the same time, the notion of human rights replaced the notion of divine authority. As it turned away from religious faith, the Enlightenment was permeated with optimism regarding human nature, reason, and scientific progress.

Each of these movements rose to greater prominence as modernity unfolded. Though most of modernity's values may have begun as discus-sions among intellectuals, they eventually became commonly accepted. These were the embedded components of the modern age.

Characteristics of the Modern Age

Enlightenment thinking sought to replace faith in God with human reason. In the minds of most Enlightenment thinkers, superstition and ignorance had prevailed during the Middle Ages. Intellectuals blamed the church for standing in the way of human progress, preaching intolerance, and blocking the light of reason. Many philosophers began to doubt whether faith and reason were even compatible.[8] Whereas the premodern challenge was to rec-oncile facts to faith, the modern challenge was to reconcile faith to the facts. If there was any serious conflict, faith was the loser.

Alongside reason, *science took on a new and important role.* Two impor-tant developments helped promote the rise of modern science.

First, inventors and discoverers began to pay more attention to observa-tion and experimentation as the means of gaining knowledge of the natural world. Though this method had been around since the time of Aristotle, people like Leonardo da Vinci, William Gilbert, and Francis Bacon found that careful, systematic experimentation and observation of actual phenom-ena yielded a useful kind of information about nature.

Second, many of the great philosophers, such as Descartes, also were mathematicians. Astronomers like Copernicus, Kepler, and Galileo used mathematics to calculate the size, distance, and movements of the planets. Modern science approached the study of objects and organisms by taking them apart, studying each individual unit, and determining how all the components worked to form the whole. As various fields of research were broken down into smaller units, specialization in specific fields became necessary to accommodate the new information.

Science was assumed to be capable of revealing the whole truth about the universe. For sickness and illness there was medicine. For communication and travel there was technology. For building bridges and skyscrapers there was engineering. In one way or another, science inserted itself into every department of modern life. The modern era became the "age of gadgets"— if science cannot address it, then it cannot be done. In the words of Bertrand Russell, "What science cannot tell us, mankind cannot know."

Science became more secular and more separated from philosophy. As science spread out into different disciplines, it became impossible for one person to maintain a thorough knowledge of both philosophy and one's specialized field. Previously, intellectuals had considered science to be a branch of philosophy. Gradually, however, scientists forgot they were "doing philosophy" and failed to see the limits of their discipline. They began to make pronouncements about all kinds of human concerns, many that did not fall within the purview of science.

With the elevation of scientific knowledge, *the inherent humanism of modernity became more prominent.* Humanism actually developed during the Renaissance, but at that time humanists were not out to replace the moral ideal of the church. To them, according to one historian, "the world had become a human world, determined (and threatened) by human aspirations…. The world may have been created by God, but it was now in the hands—for better or worse—of humanity."[9] The humanism of modernity, however, became more and more secular. Eventually, the full development of a human being (rationally, artistically, morally), which was a central concern for rational thinkers, was considered too important to be left in the hands of the church.[10]

The smallest unit in society is a single individual. That sentence may seem obvious, but it was not obvious in premodern times. In many societies, the family was the smallest unit of society. People did not think in terms of themselves alone but in terms of the health and safety of their families or clans. The individual existed only as a member of a larger unit. But modernity stressed the value of an independent and individual self—individual potential, individual achievement, and individual freedom.[11]

Modernity and God

With the rise of the modern era, people influenced by the currents in modern thought could no longer look at God in the same way. Hostility toward Christianity grew, and many scholars preserved the memory of Galileo's persecution by Roman Catholic authorities as an instance of religion suppressing the free inquiry of a scientific mind. Research moved in a secular context as the role of God receded from laboratory-type thinking and experimentation. Philosophers became more and more bold in their conviction that God's existence could not be proved either scientifically or rationally.

If the dangers and challenges of postmodernity seem terrifying, it might be helpful to remember the intense hostility of the modern era toward Christianity. Modernity might seem to be more religion-friendly than postmodernity. If so, one analyst argues, that is due only to the fact that "despite the naturalism which came increasingly to the fore [after the Renaissance], the new culture remained for several centuries stubbornly Christian."[12] In time, however, that stubbornness wore off and modernity's memory of traditional Christianity continued to fade.

In the mid-1960s—perhaps the twilight of modernity—Harvard professor Harvey Cox published *The Secular City,* which quickly became a best-selling book. In Cox's view, the secular city was modern society at its zenith, where the "idea of God" was superfluous. "The forces of secularization have no serious interest in persecuting religion. Secularization simply bypasses and undercuts religion and goes on to other things."[13]

Any religious impulse that still survived in the secular city could be met or managed by the new team of caregivers, with therapists acting as priests—listening to our confessions and giving us reassurances about our lovableness—and scientists acting as community shamans whose knowledge of the universe holds the promise of all cures. Was "Mr. Wizard" not a shaman of sorts? And what about Bill Nye, "the Science Guy"?

Science and Faith

One evening, a women's prayer meeting had taken over our house, so my oldest son and I headed outside to explore the neighborhood. *Time* magazine had recently published an article that argued strongly for Darwinian evolution and hinted at the lack of sophistication of fundamentalist Christians who still believed in creationism.

I was helping guide William and his tricycle across a driveway when we nearly bumped into an old man out for a walk. We chatted a bit, and when he asked what I did for a living, I told him I was a minister. Then he asked if I had seen the article in *Time.* "I suppose a lot of people will be throwing their Bibles away after they read that," he said.

"Only if they haven't read them," I replied, "and if they don't know any more about science than the article contained." The old man grunted and continued on his way. His conclusion—and that of modernism—was that science filled every space that God would have otherwise occupied.

Perhaps it was inevitable that modernity's infatuation with science would lead to a new form of biblical study—not the reverent search for

God's revealed truth but a critical analysis of the Bible as literature. As a matter of fact, no other historical document was ever, or has ever, been subjected to as much scrutiny. Since faith had been pushed aside, there was nothing to prevent scholars from looking at the Bible as they would any secular document. More interest was given to the human authors, the historical-cultural context, and the study of its language than to its divine inspiration and living message.

To be fair, the modern era developed tools for biblical study and research that have uncovered rich insights into the meaning of Scripture. The scientific analysis to which the Bible was subjected yielded a more reliable, tested, and true Scripture for the modern era, but the cost was great. The dynamic impact that Scripture once had in people's lives and society as the divine Word of God was diminished.

If we were to sum up in one word modernism's scientific attitude toward God, we would probably use the familiar term coined by Thomas Huxley: *agnosticism*. Huxley—known as "Darwin's bulldog" and a classic example of the modern mind—believed it was wrong for people to say they were certain about anything they could not prove logically and scientifically. As far as he was concerned, this standard for certainty ruled out the possibility of taking traditional theology seriously. Since theological statements cannot be scientifically proven or disproved, humans could not know about such things as God, immortality, and the supernatural.[14] If God existed, He was at best unknowable.

A Failed Christian Response

The church's influence and status in the world gradually diminished. As a result, the church typically was left out of important discussions while the voice of its intellectual competitors—reason, skepticism, and science—grew stronger.

Why did Christians fail to oppose these forces and fight to maintain the church's prominence? Why were Christians not more active in addressing these issues? I can think of four reasons that help explain the ineffective Christian response to modernism. Each one has particular relevance to the church today.

The overconfidence of the church prevented its leaders from recognizing the threat. The church's role had been so strong in Western culture that many of the clergy assumed the church simply would continue to enjoy its same privileged status. After all, the church was the institution that preserved tradition, and where would society be without tradition? What they did not realize is that tradition was one of the ideas under attack. Maybe they assumed God would not allow the church to be superseded by any human contrivance.

The irrelevance of the church's response made its attempts to influence intellectuals ineffective. There were preachers who did address the rising tide of rationalism and a few Christian philosophers who argued for coexistence between faith and reason. However, many preachers used premodern strategies on a battlefield that was increasingly modern. They used a heavy-handed and intimidating mix of argumentation, Scripture quotations, hellfire sermons, and mockery of secular philosophers. But those arguments failed to answer the challenge of modernity in modernity's terms.

The gradual slippage of the church was almost imperceptible, at least at the beginning. Few people recognized the need to take up arms and enter the battle until it was too late. Many early modern philosophers, such as Pascal and Descartes, were devout believers, as were many early scientists. Indeed, in the twentieth century intellectuals questioned whether modern science would have been possible apart from the Judeo-Christian worldview (i.e., the belief that the universe is ordered and open to rational investigation because of the design and intelligence of its Creator). Protestant reformers also contributed to the rise of the modern age, but they could not have possibly predicted how their revolutionary thinking would fuel the humanism that was on the rise.

The church underestimated the long-range impact of the philosophical changes taking place. After all, one had to be well-read to follow the philosophical debates and developments, and much of society still was illiterate. Thus it seemed far-fetched that ideas like David Hume's radical empiricism and skepticism would ever become doctrines for the masses. The church simply was not able to see how ripe the world was for change. Eventually the new thinking of the intellectuals (reinforced by science, medicine, and technology) spread throughout modern society and won the mind of the general public.

Even though the church "came late to the party," it finally entered the modern world. Though it never regained its former prominence, the church worked hard to catch up with modernity while it continued to be treated like an unwanted stepchild in most academic and intellectual circles.

In time the church built modern seminaries, adopted the modern worldview, and produced an impressive array of apologetics to answer modern skepticism and defend a rational faith. Conservative theologians became skilled in demonstrating the "reasonableness" of Christianity.

But now the whole structure of modernism is breaking down, and its objections to religious belief have lost their power. We are witnessing the exhaustion of the ideas and dreams that produced the modern age. It would seem that just as Christians are arriving on the playing field of modernity, carrying their bats, gloves, and baseballs, everyone else has switched to soccer.

The End, or a New Beginning?

When my son Michael was about five years old, I took him rock climbing in the Joshua Tree National Monument. We had scrambled over the easier trail beneath us, but now we were inching our way along the face of a rock with a long, steep drop to the rocks below. (It was a scary climb but not difficult, and he was in no danger.) Just before we were about to pull ourselves over the top, Michael asked me, "Dad, couldn't we just stay home and not do dangerous things?"

Some Christians feel the same way about postmodernity. They see obvious dangers in the road ahead and wonder if we cannot opt to stay in modernity. Though it might not be friendly to Christianity, at least we know our way around. But this time we have no choice. The world is moving forward, and it won't stop and wait for the church to catch up.

We really are not in a position to choose between modernity and postmodernity. Even if we could choose, it would be an extremely difficult decision, since neither worldview is grounded in biblical revelation. Both systems present positive and negative conditions that function for and against Christian faith. If we are *in* our culture, yet not *of* it, then postmodernity is our new home because that is where our culture is located. Besides, if this is where God wants us, then it is because He knows we will do our best work for Him here.

However, we do need some assurance that our faith is not going to be dismantled or set adrift on an ocean of relativism. We have to know that when we climb out of bed in the morning, the world will not have altered so much that there is no longer any room for a Creator or creatures who believe in Him. We need to know that the Bible is still true, our faith in God still works, and there are rewards for choosing good and a price to pay for choosing evil.

In Psalm 11, David asks, "When the foundations are being destroyed, what can the righteous do?" The rest of this book will explore the answer to that question. The foundations of what seemed a stable culture for the last two hundred years have been shaken. For direction on what we need to do, let's consider more wisdom from Psalm 11.

"In the LORD I take refuge. How then can you say to me: 'Flee like a bird to your mountain'" (verse 1). The stability and security we desire is found in God. There is no need for us to waste energy trying to flee the challenges of our world. In every difficulty, threat, and heartache we find shelter in God. Taking refuge in God is a realistic and desirable option for postmodern men and women.

"The LORD is in his holy temple; the LORD is on his heavenly throne" (verse 4). There is a reality that is not shaken by the culture-quakes that rattle this world, a stable foundation that will never collapse, namely, God's throne, which is not located in transient cultures. God's throne is heavenly and eternal, and it lies outside our world of change. The throne is not only a symbol of authority and stability, but it is the place where justice is administered. So no matter what changes take place in the human realm, the wicked still will be punished and the righteous still will receive their reward (verse 7).

There is a way to maintain our orientation to God's throne and live in the postmodern world at the same time. In fact, it is our orientation to His throne that enables us to navigate these uncharted waters. "Your throne was established long ago; you are from all eternity" (Psalm 93:2). And He will continue to all eternity.

Our worlds change, "For here we do not have an enduring city" (Hebrews 13:14). However, God's changeless Word enters into every time and culture with compelling relevance and the hope of salvation. In Scripture we frequently are reminded of the transience of our world and the permanence of God's Word (see, for instance, Matthew 24:35 and 1 John 2:15-17). The Bible still is our guide, God still rules, and the promise still is certain: If we lead upright lives we "will see his face" (Psalm 11:7).

Chapter 2

THE UNRAVELING OF MODERNITY

*These are the numbers of the men armed for battle
who came to David at Hebron...men of Issachar,
who understood the times and knew what Israel should do.*

1 CHRONICLES 12:23,32

In 1826 a Frenchman by the name of Joseph Niépce set on his window sill a special box he had made. He attached a metal plate inside the back of the box and coated it with a chemical that reacted to light. He left his box on the window sill for eight hours. When he opened it, he found imprinted on the metal plate a fuzzy image of the world outside his window. This was an early attempt at photography.

A few years later another French inventor took the process a step further. He coated a copper plate with silver, then "took a picture" by exposing the plate to a still life. Next he used mercury vapors to develop the image and table salt to set and protect his picture. With this method he was able to get a much clearer reproduction than Niépce's. Other innovations that followed included light-sensitive paper and lenses engineered especially for taking pictures. In 1888 George Eastman developed the Kodak box camera and turned photography into a commodity.

Photography not only represented a major technological advance, it also had a dramatic effect on the world of art and eventually on the way people viewed representations of reality. Before the development of photographic images, visual representations of the world were produced through painting, sculpture, and woodcut engraving. Artists strove for realism in their work, the faithful reproduction of what they could see with their eyes. Everyone who viewed a painter's work, no matter where they lived or in what time, could see the world as it was captured by the artist's brushes and paint.

But if a photograph could represent the same scene as a painting with equal or even greater clarity, what further need did we have for realistic paintings? As the technology of photography became more and more sophisticated, there was less need for paintings of the "real" world.[1] Modern art broke from the mimetic tradition (imitation) of classical art. Rather than try to produce a "copy" of what was out there in the real world, artists invented new forms of art, like abstract painting, cubism, dadaism, and surrealism.[2]

If you tend to scratch your head when you hear that an abstract painting sold for the price of a small nation, don't feel ashamed. This is the nature of much modern art, literature, and music. The work of modern artists became so difficult to understand that they created a split between highbrow and lowbrow culture and required specialists and critics to explain it to nonspecialist observers. On the other hand, if you cannot see the beauty, pathos, and depth of Picasso's *Guernica*, then you might think about taking an art-appreciation class.

Having been liberated from the constraints of representation, artists were free to explore the relationships of form and color or to express their own psychological experience of perceiving an object rather than trying to reproduce it. Their random splashes and dribbles of paint on a canvas often reflected their mood rather than their model. For a while there still was a

28

world out there that artists could perceive and to which they could respond, but later the very notion of realism (belief in a reality) was abandoned.[3]

By the late sixties and early seventies, avant-garde artists were ready to push beyond modernism. The term *postmodern* was adopted to describe a new movement in art and architecture. The term soon became useful for describing changes in many other fields, to the extent that it has come to permeate discussions on almost every subject. According to one writer, "One of the great strengths of the word, and the concept, and why it will be around for another hundred years, is that it is carefully suggestive about our having gone beyond the worldview of modernism—which is clearly inadequate—without specifying where we are going. That is why people will spontaneously use it, as if for the first time."[4]

The Disappearance of Reality

What distinguishes the modern from the postmodern is more a matter of philosophy than style. "A postmodern artist or writer," according to French philosopher Jean-François Lyotard, "is in the position of a philosopher."[5] In modern art the work is not representative of the real world. It may even reflect simply a feeling, such as the artist's emotional response to nothingness. In postmodern art there is no real world. It is held that *nothing exists beyond the piece of art*, hence there is nothing to represent. The piece represents itself, is its own reality, and that is all. Therefore, postmodern art tends to be self-conscious, playful, and ironic.[6] In postmodernity, reality disappears, and all that is left is the counterfeit, the image, the piece of art that relates to nothing.

We might be tempted to think that any philosopher who argued against the existence of reality should be put out to pasture. But if you follow the movements of philosophy that lead to this conclusion, you find that it is intellectually defensible. Reality, according to postmodernism, is something that cultures construct or manufacture, and people within a particular culture accept its perception of reality without question. At least until they bump up against other cultures, which is happening all the time nowadays. And that is why a sense of loss of reality pervades society.

One of the themes of postmodernity is the pluralism of our age (i.e., accepting the fact that many cultures exist and believing they are all of equal value). Postmodern art, therefore, often takes the form of a pastiche or collage, a combination of styles drawn from history as well as from a variety of contemporary cultures. Exhibits of contemporary art often display a wide diversity of styles in a single showing, and one piece of art may incorporate several different styles. The loss of reality removes any hierarchy of values that might otherwise place one style above another. If there is no reality against which we might evaluate the "truthfulness" of a work of art, then all styles are created equal.

As in postmodern art, so also in postmodern architecture there is an intentional combining of old and new, functional and ornamental, domestic and foreign, which allows viewers a variety of ways to interpret what they see. A famous example of this is the AT&T building designed by Philip Johnson in New York City. At first it looks like one more glass and steel skyscraper, rectangular and tall. But it is topped with a Chippendale broken pediment that makes it look like a huge grandfather clock. The building is a nostalgic reminder of the past and at the same time a modern skyscraper. It playfully mimics, yet mocks, the skyscrapers that surround it.

An important feature of modern architecture was its insistence on utilizing new technologies, new materials, and new methods of construction to create a building that was engineered to be both stable and functional. In contrast, postmodern architecture is not obsessed with the newest and latest but works just as easily with nonfunctional decoration borrowed from the past as it does with high-tech engineering.

The New Values

If we were to utilize a modern era mind-set to outline the distinctive features of postmodern art, the following characteristics would stand out. Each of these carries an influence that goes far beyond the world of art.

Postmodern art is marked by *a multiplicity of style.*

Postmodern art is *self-referential.* Unlike classical art's use of symbols that point to transcendent truths, postmodern art does not point to a reality beyond itself. Instead, it conspicuously draws attention to itself.

Postmodern art *makes no attempt to hide the fact that it is contrived,* that it is a human product and the artist establishes the boundaries of reality for the composition within the space it occupies (i.e., the canvas). As Zygmunt Bauman observes in *Intimations of Postmodernity,* postmodern art is "blatantly and emphatically *construed.*"[7]

Postmodern art *challenges authority.* Who determines what is art and what is not? Who determines what is high art and what is popular art? What academies, institutions, or elite societies are responsible for labeling art? Whatever they are, they represent power structures that unfairly oppress people who work outside the established system. Postmodern art seeks to "unbalance" such power structures. Theologian Stanley Grenz explains, "Postmodern artists don't view stylistic diversity merely as a means to grab attention. The attraction is deeper than that. It's part of a more general postmodern attitude, a desire to challenge the power of modernity as invested in institutions and canonical traditions."[8]

This admittedly oversimplified review highlights three themes that characterize all of postmodernity:

- *pluralism* (expressed in eclecticism, combining a variety of historical, ethnic, and artistic styles)

- *a suspicion of realism* (a rejection of the idea that anything exists other than the work itself)
- *an undermining of authority*

Beyond art, however, modernism also lost vigor in the fields of literature, philosophy, politics, and culture. It's important to examine this decline in order to understand how disillusionment with modernism prepared the way for postmodernism.

Modernity's Failed Dreams

One of Disneyland's featured attractions in the sixties was the Carousel of Progress located in Tomorrowland and sponsored by General Electric. As the circular building rotated around a central structure, guests were treated to visions of the future revealed on a series of stationary stages where electrical appliances, gadgets, and labor-saving devices promised a technological utopia. And while the theater swung around to the next stage, the theme song blared from hidden speakers: "There's a great big, beautiful tomorrow / shining at the end of every day." This anthem expressed the very heart of modernity's optimism, based on the advance of science and the blessings—"just a dream away"—that it would bestow on humankind.

Flash forward to the eighties and nineties, and a very different picture of the future emerges. Movies from that period portrayed cynical heroes who, having given up on the quest for meaning, learned to survive in a dark and dirty world, molding under a continuous, toxic drizzle. The unqualified optimism of modernity gave way to a skeptical and emotionally detached resignation to the inevitable consequences of ozone depletion, overpopulation, pollution, government corruption, multiculturalism (not in a glorified "melting pot" but in a blurring of language and ethnicity into a bleak monoculture), and degeneration of civilization. Technology in these movies provides benign service to humans, but it is also a potential threat, if not an outright evil. Which future seems most plausible from today's perspective, Disneyland's optimistic Tomorrowland or the movie *Blade Runner*? Modernity had promised a universal Disneyland, but it failed to deliver.

According to one observer, "Postmodernism grew out of disillusionment with modernism's failure to produce a perfect, rational, planned, and compassionate world. The dreams of modernity were admirable but in the light of contemporary history seem naive."[9] The dream of a "great big, beautiful tomorrow" has been shattered, and with it, the foundation of modernity.   *dystopia*

The modern age is wobbling because modernity made promises it could not keep. The foundations of modern society are being destroyed as technology and the knowledge industry it created undermine its chief premises. In *Christian Belief in a Postmodern World*, Diogenes Allen cites evidence of the breakdown of the modern mentality in at least four areas. We'll look at the collapse of these four pillars of modernism, the collapse that caused the modern age to fall apart.[10]

Four Pillars of Modernism

Pillar One: Reason Is Superior to Faith

The horrific massacre of students at Columbine High School in Littleton, Colorado, in April 1999 was not a drug-related or gang-related incident in a high-crime neighborhood. It occurred in mainstream, middle-class culture. In the pain and frustration people felt immediately afterward, the cannon of blame was pointed in every direction: the NRA, poor parenting, depictions of violence in movies and video games, and access to hate sites on the Internet. Some Christians also blamed the bureaucrats who, they said, "took God out of our schools"—a theologically weak accusation, to say the least. It's a very small and powerless God indeed who can be told where He can and cannot go.

But how do we explain a tragedy such as Columbine? A variety of factors can unhinge an adolescent's mind and remove the inhibition against taking a human life. But underneath those factors lies the fact that it is extremely difficult to teach morals in a godless context. By the same token, a *Book of Virtues* is powerless to change notions of right and wrong—let alone a person's behavior—if it appears in a moral vacuum. And that is what modernism created in society, a moral vacuum that science and philosophy have not been able to fill. In respect to morality, modernity shot itself in the foot when it replaced faith with reason.

Ever since the Enlightenment, science and reason promised to answer all the important questions regarding the universe, truth, and meaning. For the first time in history, theologians were viewed as quaint representatives of an irrelevant, mythic, and old-fashioned religion. Christianity was perceived as harmless at best and the enemy of society, science, and progress at worst. The Bible came under the attack of scientific analysis and was treated as a primitive and entirely human document. Under the weight of modernity's rigid definition of the laws of nature, miracles were dismissed as pious fictions and the biblical stories were nothing but ancient myths.

These modern innovations would have appeared absurd to most philosophers living prior to the Enlightenment. "Augustine in the fifth century did not think the Bible was out-of-date," according to theologian Ted Peters. "Nor did Thomas Aquinas in the twelfth century or Martin Luther and John Calvin in the sixteenth century think of the Bible as old-fashioned. Only those who come after the rise of natural science and the Enlightenment pit what scripture says against what we learn from other sources. This distancing of ourselves from what was said in the ancient world of the Bible is due to a fundamental shift in our way of thinking, a shift that marks the difference between the premodern and the modern eras."[11]

As the modern era rose, it bore the promise of providing better explanations for the nature and origin of the universe than those provided by religion. Some rationalists believed religion would be the last vestige of superstition to be buried by reason in the graveyard of obsolescence.

Modernism so thoroughly penetrated society that people can go through school, read daily newspapers and periodicals, work in large corporations, serve in political offices and never learn that God has any relevance to real life. The boast of the modern age was that the world no longer needed God.

Today, however, modernity no longer holds hope for certainty, and resignation to uncertainty has eroded the modern promise. More important, however, is the fact that the question of God and the Bible cannot be seriously excluded from discussion about the universe and the possible meaning of human existence. Current issues in science—quantum theory, chaos theory, Heisenberg's uncertainty principle—raise questions that cannot exclude God as one possible answer.

According to Christian philosopher Diogenes Allen,

> It can no longer be claimed that philosophy and science have
> established that we live in a self-contained universe.... This radical change has been independently reinforced by recent developments in science, especially in cosmology.... In both fields the
> questions arise, Why does the universe have this particular order,
> rather than another possible one? and Why does the universe
> exist? The questions point toward God as an answer. As we shall
> see, it is beyond the capacity of those fields of inquiry to make a
> positive pronouncement on the matter. All they can say is that
> the order and existence of the universe pose real questions that

they cannot answer and recognize that God is the sort of reality that would answer them.[12]

Science is still in the business of answering questions, but there are now scientists who concede that some questions cannot be adequately addressed by science alone. Of course, not all scientists are prepared to accept this limitation. Patrick Glynn has observed that "Many scientists are profoundly uncomfortable with the universe of the new cosmology, precisely because it leaves such ample room for God. The whole picture is damnably disconcerting: a universe with a beginning, designed for man. Many scientists want this picture to go away."[13] But it is not likely to go away because the course of history is generating new conversations that must at least remain open to the idea of God.

Pillar Two: Science Will Lead to Morality

In 1969 a young scientist coauthored a book that supported the orthodox view of modern science: that living organisms evolved from inorganic chemicals. *Biochemical Predestination* became one of the two best-selling advanced-level books on chemical evolution. However, in October 1992 this same scientist, Dean Kenyon, professor of biology at San Francisco State University, was called into a meeting with the department chairman. Kenyon had broken one of the unwritten rules of the biology department when he suggested to his students the limitations of Darwinian evolution and asked them to consider evidence for "intelligent design" in the universe. He was ordered to stop teaching this view in his beginning-level biology classes immediately.

Later Kenyon was accused of teaching religion instead of science and was prohibited from teaching his introductory biology course altogether. He claims he never taught religion, saying the discussions were strictly based on science and that he simply gave the standard presentation of evolution, followed by his own doubts that emerged when searching for evidence to support it.

In 1993 the university's Academic Freedom Committee investigated Kenyon's case and ruled in his favor. Nevertheless, the biology department still refused to let him teach his introductory class, even though he had been exonerated. In December of that year the faculty senate voted to reinstate him. Later that month the head of the biology department gave in, and Kenyon was permitted to return to his lectures.

Dean Kenyon has been a pioneer in the field of biophysics, and his credentials are outstanding. But because he came to see evidence of intelligent design in the universe, his colleagues attempted to excommunicate him from introductory classes in biology. His scientific view challenged the science department's dogma. Do you suppose we will see a rise of scientific fundamentalism in the science community if its monopoly in society continues to slip?

The controversy surrounding Professor Kenyon reflects modernity's rejection of absolute values and divine revelation. If humans needed a set of moral values, they could "discover" them through science and reason, in a way similar to the discovery of vaccines for viruses. This secular quest for morality persisted into the twentieth century. A classic example is that of the humanist and psychologist Abraham Maslow who suggested a naturalistic set of values derived from scientific research rather than religious doctrine. His words today almost look like the script of a "B" science fiction movie.

According to Maslow,

> We can no longer rely on tradition, on consensus, on cultural
> habit, on unanimity of belief to give us our values. These agreed-
> upon traditions are all gone. Of course, we never should have
> rested on tradition—as its failures must have proven to everyone
> by now—it never was a firm foundation. It was destroyed too

easily by truth, by honesty, by the facts, by science, by simple,
pragmatic historical failure.

Only truth itself can be our foundation, our base for building. Only empirical, naturalistic knowledge, in its broadest
sense, can serve us now."[14]

Interestingly, Maslow clung to this optimistic view of empirical, naturalistic knowledge despite the fact that the "very modern" twentieth century
produced Nazi Germany, Imperialist Japan, the Soviet Union, Communist
China, and two world wars—the most destructive of all eras in human history.

Can science alone provide humans with a worthy set of moral values?
Here is another area where modernity has failed. Steven Weinberg, winner
of the 1979 Nobel Prize in Physics, presents an honest assessment of the
limitations of the natural sciences. In *Dreams of a Final Theory*, he states,
"Judging from this historical experience, I would guess that, though we shall
find beauty in the final laws of nature, we will find no special status for life
or intelligence. A fortiori, we will find no standards of value or morality.
And so we will find no hint of any God who cares about such things. We
may find these things elsewhere, but not in the laws of nature."[15]

Coming at the end of the modern era from a world-renown scientist,
this inescapable conclusion may be the last word on modernism's attempt to
arrive at moral values by way of science and reason alone. The "new superstition," which is now being rejected by postmodernists, is the notion that
science can answer the ultimate human questions of meaning, truth, good-
ness, and so on. In a 1984 interview, neurobiologist John Eccles said,

Unfortunately, many scientists and interpreters of science don't
understand the limits of the discipline. They claim much more
for it than they should. They argue that someday science will
explain values, beauty, love, friendship, aesthetics, and literary
quality. They say, "All of these will eventually be explicable in

terms of brain performance. We only have to know more about the brain." That view is nothing more than a superstition that confuses both the public and many scientists.

My task as a scientist is to try to eliminate superstitions and to have us experience science as the greatest human adventure. But to understand is not to completely explain. Understanding leaves unresolved the great features and values of our existence.[16]

Eccles claims there are limits to science that leave unanswered many important questions. He denies that "religion and science are necessarily at odds" and describes himself as a "practicing Christian." But the point is clear: Modernism failed to make good on its promise to provide humans a basis for morality on science and reason alone. Therefore another pillar of the modern age has toppled.

Pillar Three: Progress Is Inevitable

The notion of a continual and upward progress to a Golden Age "has reached something of a dead end," to borrow a phrase from Christopher Lasch. "As the twentieth century draws to a close, we find it more and more difficult to mount a compelling defense of the idea of progress; but we find it equally difficult to imagine life without it."[17]

Through most of the modern period, optimism about "human progress" has been strong, almost euphoric. Human wisdom and invention would ultimately cure all diseases and tame all wildernesses, creating a paradise on earth. "Science was to become the great redemptive force! And, within science, chemistry was to become the chief instrument whereby human misery would be reduced and new marvels created."[18]

The modern era certainly has witnessed an awesome and impressive parade of technological advances. There's no doubt that our lives and health are much improved due to the continuous progress in medicine, immunology, transportation, and so on. But along with these improvements there also have been a terrifying proliferation of painful consequences and by-products, as well as a means of mass destruction and genocide more effective than any that were dreamed of in earlier ages.

The nature of science is such that it cannot help but forge ahead into better understanding of and models for our universe, but scientists have little or no control regarding how their technology will be used. Even simple technology can be misused to demolish a downtown Federal Building in Oklahoma or to poison Japanese subway commuters. Technology is not all bad, but no one can deny the devastation and widespread misery of a Chernobyl-type disaster. Few people today see technology as the world's messiah, here to meet our deepest needs. And many people view the mutant, corrosive, polluting by-products of technology as responsible for decreasing the beauty and quality of life on our planet. Thus we hear the echoes of another pillar of modernism as it comes crashing down.

Pillar Four: Knowledge Is Inherently Good

Some years ago on a warm summer evening, a couple invited me to their home for dinner. While enjoying some downtime together, we turned on the television and happened to catch a documentary on Albert Einstein and his role in developing the first atomic bomb. No sooner was "the bomb" manufactured than Einstein was busy sending messages to Washington begging the president and his advisors not to use atomic weapons or ever unleash their destructive power. For the rest of his life he regretted having anything to do with the development of the atom bomb.

The modern era was infatuated with knowledge and information. Thus the quest of research in all fields was energized by the belief that the results would be beneficial to human life. We have learned in this century, however, that information can be used in ways that are morally irresponsible and incredibly destructive. Recent advances in unlocking the genetic code have raised public concerns over who has the right to patent human genes or gene strands and what kind of limitations should be placed on research laboratories in manipulating those genes.

According to some analysts, bioethics will become an even greater issue in the next few decades due to continuing development of biological and genetic engineering, especially as it relates to the Human Genome Project. The more mysteries we unlock in our DNA, the more we will question what it means biologically to be human and what significance should be attached to one particular human being with his or her own characteristic physical and psychological features and idiosyncrasies. We should also remember that much of the motivation for the continued advance of knowledge in almost every field is to serve military interests or consumer desire—i.e., for the perfect body or the perfect baby.

The modern age applauded scientific knowledge and held in high esteem the men and women who wore the white lab coats. The voice of science was privileged in public discussion, that is, it was given greater credence and respect than voices from other fields, be they literary, religious, philosophical, or aesthetic.

The prestige of science is diminishing though, and most people feel a certain amount of ambivalence toward the unlimited acquisition and distribution of knowledge. We would love to discover a cure for cancer, AIDS, and even more trivial problems such as baldness and acne. On the other hand we fear the possibility that some wide-eyed physicist may attempt to clone himself in a secret laboratory or a radical terrorist group may be able to deliver a nuclear or biological weapon of mass destruction to the heart of our nation. We also are concerned that our children can click their way into the Internet and learn how to engage in occult rituals, synthesize mind-altering drugs from common household products, join a hate group, or commit suicide. The reverberations of another pillar falling to the ground announce a serious error in the modern mentality.

What Does God Want Now?

Wisdom dictates that we be aware of the times and act accordingly. Changes in our world require us to adopt new ways of living.

At thirty years old, David the shepherd could finally stop living like an outlaw constantly on the run. He moved to Hebron where he was crowned king of Judah. Soon there were contingents of soldiers coming to him from each of the tribes of Israel. Among the arriving caravans and troops were the men of Issachar. Like some of the others who had already come, these men had a special talent: They "understood the times and knew what Israel should do" (1 Chronicles 12:32). Their first skill was the ability to decipher the important political, economic, and spiritual currents of the time in which they lived. Their second skill was the ability to produce a strategy that made the best use of their time (or season). They hoped for a positive outcome in the future, but it depended on their insight, decisions, and actions within the present.

No doubt the "men of Issachar" are a rare breed. For at least two hundred years Christians have not done well in discerning the times or knowing what to do. Cries for another Reformation, Great Awakening, or Pentecost imply that the answer to today's challenges lies in the past. The Reformation was the answer to the abuses of sixteenth century Roman Catholicism, the Great Awakenings fit the rational context of modernism, and as for Pentecost, well, that was a unique event.

We need to discover what God wants to do in *our* century. Theologian Ray Anderson argues that the "Spirit that comes to the church comes out of the future, not the past. The presence of the Spirit is the anticipation of the return of Christ." Therefore, rather than constantly ask, "How was it done before?" Christians need to ask, "How does the Spirit want to work now?" Anderson says we can expect the Spirit to "prepare the church to be the church that Christ desires to see when he returns, not the one that he left in the first century."[19] This is exactly what the church needs today: the guidance and power of the Holy Spirit to help us understand these postmodern times and know what to do.

Chapter 3

GETTING A HANDLE ON POSTMODERNITY

For all of you who were baptized into Christ
have clothed yourselves with Christ.
There is neither Jew nor Greek, slave nor free, male nor female,
for you are all one in Christ Jesus.

GALATIANS 3:27-28

In 1972 I was single and carefree. Three buddies and I combined our life savings and rented a motor home so we could cruise up the California coast looking for opportunities to evangelize and teach Bible studies. Two of my friends were musicians, and I was a fledgling preacher. After brief engagements in Lompoc and Cambria, we decided to drive up to San Simeon and tour Hearst Castle.

The beautiful, manicured grounds of what was formerly the property of newspaper mogul William Randolph Hearst gave us the feeling of walking through a dream world where Greek mythology and European fairy tales collided. The sheer opulence of the "castle" and its furnishings was overwhelming. As our guide drew our attention to various features of the architecture, she repeatedly said they represented a "wonderful blend of the old and the new." In other words, old-world styles and ornaments were placed within a modern framework. Her "wonderful blend of old and new" seemed to be a contrived way of saying that this eccentric tycoon ransacked European estates for pillars, mantels, sculptures, and furniture that caught his fancy and had his contractor slap them together to show them off without the "castle" collapsing underneath their weight.

The effect was not altogether unlike shanties in the desert constructed of plywood, refrigerator doors, cardboard boxes, canvas covers, and old tires—same concept, different budget. Contrasting architectural touches were added simply because they were beautiful, but there was no overarching plan or design. Touring Hearst Castle was similar to riding a tram through a movie lot where time periods and world geographies pass in rapid succession; you enter a new era simply by turning a corner.

Likewise, postmodernity combines "the old and the new," not in an attempt to produce a "wonderful blend" but rather in a playful irony that tends to flatten the chain of command, undermine power structures, and invent new realities. Unlike modernity, postmodernism rejects the integrity of a single style. And postmodernism makes no promises about a utopian future. In fact, most expressions of postmodernity anticipate only a bleak and meaningless future that generally is approached with indifference and resignation. Some dreamers on the political left can imagine an egalitarian world, but there is nothing like a utopian society beckoning on the postmodern horizon. The future of postmodernity is *dystopia*—a word scholars like to use to describe the dysfunctional world of postmodernism.[1]

Just What Is Postmodernity?

Postmodernists like to say they are part of a movement that defies definition. After all, the urge to assign labels and to put things in neat categories is a holdover from modernity, not an aspect of postmodernity. However, at least one definition is entirely accurate: Postmodernity is that which follows modernity. The *post* suggests something that grows out of the past but is different from it. The past is never left behind completely but is taken up into the present, even if the present diverges from it or rebels against past traditions.[2] Postmodernity makes use of history, but it neither makes a clean break from the past nor looks for examples from which lessons can be learned. Instead, postmodernism borrows from both the premodern and modern ages, carefully selecting items from the past to create its own lessons.

In the last three decades we have witnessed a proliferation of "posties" (so dubbed by Charles Jenks): in philosophy, poststructuralism and postfoundationalism; in art, Post-Impressionism and postmodernism; in sociology, postindustrialism and postcapitalism (Peter Drucker); and in religion, post-Christian (Francis Schaefer). So when we turn to culture as a whole, we see that modernism—with its optimistic promises, its overconfidence in rationalism and science, its naive trust in knowledge and progress—is no longer the dominant theme. This opens the door for a postmodern culture.

Aside from the fact that it is what comes after modernism, the term *postmodernism* is difficult to define. It is possible to pick your way through a library hoping to find a book that will clarify postmodernism only to go away more confused than when you began. For this reason—and at the risk of scholarly criticism—I will set down a simple outline of postmodernity. Several themes stand out, and the key feature of each one is its place in time—the fact that it comes *after* something else.

What Is Postmodernity "After"?

Postmodernity is what comes after we all stop thinking like engineers (i.e., rationalism). Postmodernity is not irrational; it simply does not believe that human reason holds all the answers to life's questions. There are other ways to know besides human reason. They include story, metaphor, feeling, experience, and intuition. Western civilization has given reason a privileged position in the quest for knowledge, but in doing so, other ways of learning—once characteristic of non-Western cultures—have been overlooked and even scorned.

By "privileging" reason, modern culture has created a bias against other cultures, thereby depriving them of power (or "voice") in the modern world. Postmodernity wants to include the different voices of ethnic and minority groups—and the voices of the non-Western world—in public discussions. Pure logic does not win as many arguments as it (supposedly) won in modernity. Postmodern people are not moved by reason alone; they also want to know how an event or object is *experienced*.

This shift from reason to experience was evident in a conversation between a young Christian apologist and a student from the nearby university. Standing outside a coffee shop, the Christian carefully deployed the strategy he had learned from reading books by Francis Schaeffer and C. S. Lewis. He forced the student to articulate his beliefs, then gently began to push him toward the logical conclusion of those beliefs. Finally, when the poor student had no more answers or arguments, the Christian dropped the net, demonstrating that Jesus offered the only rational way out of the labyrinth. But the entire program of the apologist, so carefully constructed and executed, was demolished when the student ended the conversation by saying, "You are probably right, but I just don't feel the same way about it that you do."

Young people are not overly impressed with reason and logic. On the other hand, they love information and have access to tons of it. They are not concerned with the accumulation of information around a central core (i.e., through a skeletal structure provided by the educational system), but they know where to go to get the information they want. In the final analysis, their decisions may have less to do with what they know than with what they feel. Logic has its place, but it is not the predominant theme.

Postmodernity is what comes after the cult of science (i.e., scientism). Because it lacks modernism's allegiance to science, it might seem that postmodernity is antagonistic toward science. But that is not really the case. Postmoderns don't reject science, they simply don't view the scientific method as the only way to approach a problem.

As in the case of rationalism, the postmodern objective is to counteract scientism's exaggerated prestige, prevent its voice from drowning out other voices, and prevent scientists from always having the last word. Rather than having the last word, science is merely one of the many voices, providing one of many possible worldviews.

Science, in general, knows only one way to discover new information, and that is the rational-empirical method. Observe, theorize, experiment, analyze, and produce a hypothesis, then continue to test the hypothesis. All of this depends on logical thinking, deductive and inductive skills, and breaking down a subject into its smallest parts to see how they function to make the whole thing work (reductionism). Postmodernity claims that there are other roads to discovery, including intuition, experience, and holism. For the postmodernist, truth sometimes emerges when observing the whole rather than the component parts.

But there are other reasons science has lost a large measure of the prestige it enjoyed in the modern era. The Greenpeace organization started as an attempt to stem the tide of ecological damage done to the planet and its wildlife (not to mention human life) that has escalated with growing world population and increasing pollution. Though not always popular or law-abiding, Greenpeace has helped call the public's attention to little-known uses of science. For example, on March 3, 1998, Delta and Pipe Land Company (a division of Monsanto), along with the United States Department of Agriculture, announced that they had received a new patent on a process to genetically alter seeds so they will yield a crop but produce a following generation of seed that is sterile. Dubbed "terminator technology" by Greenpeace, this would prevent farmers from producing extra seeds for replanting or sharing with neighbors. All farmers would be forced to buy new seeds every season. Monsanto and the USDA are seeking to secure patents on their process in eighty-seven other countries. Yet many poor farmers worldwide depend on second-generation seed for planting new crops in consecutive years.

Organizations such as Greenpeace exist because science and those who wield its awesome power are no longer considered forces that are friendly toward life on earth.

Postmodernity is what comes after we have given up the belief that there is a goal, a flow, or a meaning to history (i.e. historicism). Postmodernity does not look to history for truth. In fact, it despairs of finding a true history. It is thought that all attempts to recount history fail to tell us what really happened but rather serve to promote the political agenda of the historian. The historian conveys her perceptions of the recorded accounts of events. "Those perceptions, even if reported faithfully, are not 'objectively true' but are the truth as perceived by that person through the bias of his language and culture," according to Tom Dixon. "Historical texts are interesting for discovering not what happened but how people's view of the world was skewed by their culture."[3]

Some postmodernists despair of history altogether, seeing it as "a creature of the modern Western nations," according to Pauline Rosenau. "As such it is said to 'oppress' Third World peoples and those from other cultures. History has no reality."[4]

Others argue that any history is nothing but a reconstruction of events that favors the views and serves the desired ends of historians. In fact, if handled in a postmodern way, history can have an important role in giving stronger representation to minorities by focusing on the excluded stories and marginalized peoples of the past. For example, "revisionists" rewrite history in order to highlight people and events that promote their position or cause. Drawing strength from Nietzsche's dictum, "There are no facts, only interpretations," they recast history in a light that favors their argument.

Postmodern history is less concerned with "big events," elite groups, or cultural champions and is more concerned with ordinary people or groups that have been oppressed or overlooked.[5] In postmodernity, history is not going anywhere. There is no "end point" to history—it is pointless. And for some scholars, postmodernity is the "end of history."

Postmodernity is what comes after we give up the notion of truth—that it actually exists outside of individual human minds, that it is universal and eternal (i.e. absolutism). In what he considered an extreme simplification, Jean-François Lyotard defined postmodernism "as incredulity toward meta-narratives." A metanarrative is a kind of story or myth that assumes universal acceptance and explains the meaning of our world and life in it. In the words of one author, metanarratives are a "global worldview." According to another, they are "overarching explanations of reality based on central organizing 'truths.'" That is, a metanarrative is a big story that makes sense out of life, history, and the universe.

Metanarratives, according to postmodern theory, are used to legitimize particular political structures, cultural preferences, and ways of life. Instead of one, grand narrative, postmodernity calls our attention to the many, varied, and local narratives of each culture or group. Each culture embraces stories (myths) that explain and justify its own social structures and help it define reality.

A culture's narrative is only one part of the story. Another component is its belief system. According to postmodernists, belief systems are not true in an absolute sense, they are constructed by human cultures. Rather than representing truth, belief systems merely serve the purposes of their society. If a group claims to base its belief system on certain absolutes, that group is appealing to a dogma that is locally accepted but not universally true.

According to this way of thinking, cultures create belief systems, which is another way of saying that people create reality. The narratives of a culture, passed down from one generation to the next, define reality for the group and help to enculturate the children into the community of adults. These stories preserve the worldview of the culture, give meaning to life, and help each person locate him/herself in society. Mythic stories explain origins, roles, customs, values, and purpose.

But if it is true, as postmodernism claims, that there is no grand, universal story and there are no absolutes, what happens to truth? "Truth is an Enlightenment value and subject to dismissal on these grounds alone," explains Pauline Rosenau. "Truth makes reference to order, rules, and values; depends on logic, rationality, and reason, all of which the postmodernists question. Attempts to produce knowledge in the modern world depend on some kind of truth claim, on the assumption that truth is essential."[6] But such is not the case in the postmodern world. For example, postmodernist John McGowan believes he must wrestle with the challenge of making political decisions "in the absence of truth."

Postmodernity is skeptical of truth—that such a thing exists or that people really know what they are talking about when they make truth claims. In the last chapter we saw how the loss of truth played a role in modernism's rejection of representation (realism) in art. If there is no reality to represent, then art cannot possibly be anything but its own reflection. The experience of postmodern art is subjective; viewers are not expected to believe it but to feel it.

At this point the Christian mind wants to shout, "But all of that is wrong! There *is* a metanarrative, and it is the *gospel.* There is absolute truth, and it is God. There is a foundation upon which we must establish our morals, values, and ethics." True, but at this point our goal is to understand postmodernity, not fight it. We cannot honestly interact with a postmodern world until we understand its ideas, values, and worldview. And if we are too hasty to draw lines in the sand, we may lose a priceless opportunity for evangelism—which I will describe in chapter 8.

Postmodernity is what comes after the universe no longer "really" exists (i.e. realism). We have already looked at the breakdown of realism in art, but postmodernism takes this loss of reality as a condition of life. The collapse of realism has actually been a long time coming. In the seventeenth century René Descartes began to question how thoughts could be related to objects. He raised issues that for the last three hundred years have kept philosophers of language busy hacking away at the tangled growth of words and their meanings. Postmodernists argue that there is so much play (loose movement) between words and their meanings that we must despair of any meaningful relationship between language and reality.

If you think this is too esoteric to be taken seriously, think again. In mid-1998 videotapes of President Clinton's defense before the Justice Department were televised, giving the American public the opportunity to watch their president equivocate over the meaning of the word *is*. While many people found his sputtering either comic or sad, it represented a classic postmodern problem with language.

In 1933 Alfred Korzybski argued that people tend to use language in a sloppy way, their language is not technically precise, and they do not try hard enough to distinguish between the real world and their perceptions of the world. (Could you guess he was a mathematician?) At the heart of the problem lies the word *is*. We say, "The sky is blue," but we mean the sky appears blue. If we think the sky really is blue, we are confusing perception with reality, which he called "identification" and anthropologists call naive realism. Premodernism made no distinction between perception and reality, but in modernism the split was complete. Korzybski felt the solution would be to devise a language structure that would be closer to objective reality. I imagine he would have found the following statement more to his liking:

"The scattering of the lower wavelengths of polychromatic light in the atmosphere makes the sky appear blue."

In postmodernity the relationship between words (as symbols or "signifiers") and reality (the "signified") has become so strained that postmodernists despair over ever coming to know the real world through signs (words, texts, art, or any other representation). This means they have given up any hope of ever knowing reality.

The loss of realism leads to a blurring of nonfiction and fiction, reality and fantasy, actual people and media-generated images, and between signs (i.e., symbols) and the reality they symbolize. In a situation like this, no distinction can be made between an event and a news report of the event, a seascape and a painting of a seascape, or a natural disaster and a book written about the natural disaster. The news report, painting, and book are all signs, and in postmodernity these signs are so far removed from what they may have been intended to represent that there is no longer any relationship between them and the truth. Thus the signs become the only reality we ever know. What you see is what is.

Before comedian and actor George Burns died, plans were being made to cast him in a movie to be produced after he passed away. In the movie a digitized George Burns would be the star. Now what is more real, a character played by George Burns in a movie or a digitally generated George Burns movie character? The digital George Burns is based on a character in other Burns movies (not the real man), so "he" is a sign of a sign.

According to Jean Baudrillard, when movies refer back to other movies, and paintings refer to other paintings, and texts refer to other texts without any connection to the real world, what you have is a simulacrum—a sign pointing to other signs, "a copy of a copy for which there is no original." Of course, none of this is surprising if reality is nothing more than a social construct, something that cultures create.

Postmodernity is what comes after people stop believing their culture is the one true culture or the best of all cultures (i.e. ethnocentrism). The word *ethnocentric* is to a culture what *egocentric* is to a person. We are ethnocentric when we judge the beliefs, values, and customs of other cultures on the basis of our own or when we place our culture at the top and all other cultures somewhere below ours. Thus "[a]n action is right or wrong as defined by one's own culture. Other ways of doing things in different cultures make sense or do not make sense in light of one's own culture."[7] But, to quote Paul Hiebert, "Ethnocentrism is a two-way street. We judge other peoples' customs as crude, and they feel the same about ours."

Hiebert notes that "Americans are often shocked at what they consider to be a lack of regard for human life in other societies. Foreigners, however, are struck by the American's inhumanity to the aged and the sick, who are sent away from friends and relatives and left to the care of strangers, and that even in death, the body and grave are prepared by strangers." This leads Hiebert to conclude that ethnocentrism "occurs wherever cultural differences are found."[8]

Postmodernity refuses to judge one culture superior to another. If all cultures have been constructed by humans, then one culture cannot be said to be better than others but merely different. Whereas in premodernity most people knew of no culture other than their own, and modernity tended to exclude the different cultures and their contribution to human knowledge, postmodernity celebrates differences. In fact, more insight is to be gained by studying these differences than by analyzing a culture by itself. Postmodernism focuses its attentions on the margins, asking questions like "What is missing? What has been neglected? What is unusual?"

In postmodern society we see a lot of borrowing from other cultures. It is not surprising to see a young woman driving her German-made car, listening to hip-hop music, with a native American dream catcher hanging from her rearview mirror and a Baha'i "one planet, one people" sticker on her car's bumper as she rushes to her organic chemistry class. The influence of her dominant culture does not force her to exclude the mythic, artistic, spiritual, and technical expressions of other cultures.

Postmodernity is what comes after we give up the pretense of cool detachment from the objects we study (i.e. objectivism). In the modern era, people believed they could view reality in a detached way. Biological, social, or historical systems could be studied and analyzed as something outside the observer. Postmodernism rejects this form of objectivism, the idea that people can be neutral toward and disconnected from a phenomenon they are studying.

As physicists have probed the atom, they have discovered that there are particles they cannot even observe without affecting them. Postmodernists argue that there is no neutral vantage point from which one can observe the behavior of physical objects or social systems. There is no place above or outside or over an environment that gives the observer an advantage over the observed. No human sits in God's chair or has His view of the world.

As we saw in an earlier chapter, postmodernism has an interesting effect on the role of "authors." An author stands over a text very much like a neutral observer, simply reporting the facts. Authors have a godlike view of the events that unfold in a story—being able to see over great stretches of time, knowing what is going on in two or three different places simultaneously. But this gives authors a privileged place over the information and people who are discussed and described—an advantage authors may consciously or unconsciously use to shape the text to their will. Postmodernity seeks to dismantle the privileged position of the author. According to postmodernity, every text says more than it appears to say, and because the author is also the author-*ity*, the text is a pretext for power.[9]

Postmodernity has devised methods to get around the intentions of the author. One such method, associated with the French philosopher Jacques Derrida, is deconstruction. Postmodern critics deconstruct the author's meaning of a text by taking the following steps:

- looking first at the author's intention
- exposing the author's assumptions
- uncovering other meanings in the text
- analyzing what has been *excluded* from the text
- subverting the intended meaning
- juggling the "center" of authority (between the author and those who have been excluded or marginalized by the text)

Recently we have heard scholars declare that deconstruction has been abandoned by the academic community. Perhaps that is true, but offshoots of deconstruction have only recently entered popular culture, and it will be some time before the effects completely disappear. The basic skepticism regarding the attempt of an author to sell her readers an ideology or point of view still is very much with us.

If the author of a text is no longer the authority for how his or her writing is to be interpreted, then readers have a more important role than the author. Postmodern readers make of the text what they will, never interpreting it the same way twice. Every text is capable of multiple interpretations.

Three More Postmodern Themes

In addition to understanding what postmodernism comes after, no discussion of postmodernity would be complete without looking at three additional themes: multiculturalism, disconnectedness, and the leveling of hierarchies.

Multiculturalism is the belief that all cultures are human inventions, and each group has the right to preserve its own heritage, customs, and worldview. A worldview (the way a culture defines reality) is central to every culture. There are Eastern worldviews, ethnic worldviews, scientific worldviews, and religious worldviews. People can even change worldviews—as often happens when confronted with new information or new technology.

Postmodernism refuses to privilege (give priority to) one culture or worldview over another. Every culture has a right to exist and pursue its own goals and embrace its own beliefs and values. Since truth has vanished, no worldview is more true than any other.

A worldview does not need to be proven logically because reason and logic are Enlightenment values that are not relevant to non-Western cultures. "What do you believe? Well, that totally contradicts what I believe. But that's okay because what is true for me may not be true for you and vice versa."

Postmodernists also have an option not available to earlier generations (except for people who suffered psychosis): If you do not like any of the available realities found in various cultures, invent your own. Walter Anderson observes, "In earlier times, the invention of cultural forms was shrouded in mystery; now it becomes, for better or worse, democratized." Not only do postmodernists invent new realities, but they also reinvent themselves as they "create new identities for themselves." Anderson adds, "The mass media make it easy to create and disseminate new structures of reality. A new reality does not have to convert the entire society; it merely has to find its buyers, get a share of the market, and locate enough customers to fill up the theater."[10]

This penchant for creating one's own reality can have tragic consequences. In the spring of 1997 a stream of eerie video images flowed across television screens around the world. A news camera moved slowly through a large home in an upscale neighborhood in Rancho Santa Fe, California. The camera roved from one room to another, sending us images of bodies lying on bunk beds, dressed identically and covered in purple shrouds. At first it looked as if it could have been a summer camp. But the disturbing news that all the members of this UFO cult had committed suicide in hopes of boarding a flying saucer produced a nauseating fascination for the video coverage. You didn't want to watch, but you couldn't turn away either.

Cult leader Marshall Applewhite was able to construct a worldview for thirty-nine people whose confidence in him cost them their lives. In video-taped interviews prior to their collective suicide, each person seemed to be able to communicate well and reflect their own thoughts. Apart from that slightly dazed look common to cult members, they appeared to be capable of rational thought. So their deaths, undertaken in a bizarre hope they would leave their earthly "containers" and be taken up into a spaceship, was unnerving. But if all realities are constructed realities, then the post-modern doctrine of tolerance requires us to permit even the Applewhites to spin their crazy utopias.

Disconnectedness, another theme of postmodernity, occurs in our lives because there is no formal relationship between the past, the present, or the future. In fact, time is considered a human invention. Each life experience occupies a discrete moment, disconnected from every other experience. When we are in one of these separate units of experience, it tends to fill our horizon, but it then quickly disappears as the next unit (or life byte) occurs. Traveling through postmodern culture is similar to world travel because it involves moving in and out of radically different cultural settings and world-views. We channel-surf our way through life, totally engrossed in the moment—until the next commercial.

The leveling of hierarchies, a final theme of postmodernity, is meant to destabilize power structures that tend to oppress people who are different. The modern method of organizing societies, schools, and institutions was through the establishment of hierarchies (i.e., bishops and priests, teachers and students, employers and employees, all arranged in authority/subordi-nate relationships according to rank). Postmodernity argues that the nature of hierarchies privileges one person or group while oppressing another. Therefore, by allowing every culture to speak in its own voice, and by assigning equal significance to every voice, postmodernity disrupts hierarchies and seeks to flatten them.

The organizational model of postmodernity is a *system* rather than a hierarchical organization. Of course, the formerly oppressive cultures and leaders (i.e. white males) must be beaten down at the same time that others are elevated to compensate for the great disparity between them. One voice must be silenced so the other voice can finally be heard.

The Speed of Change

We would be naive to think that major cultural changes have not occurred in other periods of time. Cultures are dynamic, thus constantly changing. What is different today is the accelerated pace of change. In the past, major changes in worldviews and customs generally took place over the span of an entire generation or even several generations. In today's world, a person can swap worldviews several times in a single life span. And postmodernists do not stop at shifting their worldviews. They also layer various (and logically contradictory) worldviews one over another.

The postmodernist is a "Protean Man," in the phrase coined by Robert Lifton, which he borrowed from the Greek god Proteus who was able to instantly change his form at will. Likewise, postmodernists are capable of shifting ideologies, politics, and religion without the slightest feeling of trauma. "Until relatively recently, no more than one major ideological shift was likely to occur in a lifetime, and that one would long be remembered as a significant turning point accompanied by profound soul-searching and conflict. But today it is not unusual to encounter several such shifts, accomplished relatively painlessly, within a year or even a month; among many groups, the rarity is a man who has gone through life holding firmly to a single ideological vision."[11]

Because of this, and other postmodern trends, today's world bears little resemblance to yesterday's world or even to the world of tomorrow. You step outside your door assuming that what worked in dealing with life yesterday will continue to be effective today. But you discover that people cannot understand you or appreciate any of your attempts to replay success strategies of the past. What has changed is not the "world outside" but our way of looking at the world. Even if you oppose the way postmodernists have redefined reality, there is little doubt that specific areas of your own thinking have been influenced by postmodern ideas.

The nature of a worldview is that it is so subtle we generally are not aware of it. We are like the machinist walking around his workbench looking for his glasses while he is already wearing them. We do not look *at* a worldview, we look *through* it. The more exposure we have to our culture— in our work environment, television, movies, books, magazines, newspapers—the more our minds are infiltrated by postmodern points of view.

Should Christians ever feel at home in a postmodern world? Can we accept the flattening of hierarchies, the equal regard for all cultures, the continuous discontinuity of journeying from one experience to the next? I believe that Jesus' prayer in John 17, in which He asks the Father to preserve His disciples and guarantee the success of their mission, has as much potency in the postmodern world as in the first century Hebraic and Hellenistic worlds. His prayer was not that the Father would "take them out of the world" but that he would "protect them from the evil one" (17:15).

If we can accept (even pray for the coming of) a kingdom where there is "neither Jew nor Greek, slave nor free, male nor female" (Galatians 3:28), then to a certain extent we can feel at home in postmodernity. There are certainly challenges and risks that confront us, and Christian believers will always be aliens and strangers in the world (Hebrews 11:13; 1 Peter 2:11). But we can also find touchstones in every culture for holding forth the truth, joy, and beauty of God's revelation. As Paul said, God has not left Himself "without testimony" (Acts 14:17).

Chapter 4

POSTMODERNISM AND POPULAR CULTURE

For God did not send his Son into the world to condemn the world,
but to save the world through him.

JOHN 3:17

My oldest daughter, Jennifer, fell in love with a young man who is a strong Christian and had at one time studied for the ministry. Of course, this made me very happy. He drove a Harley Davidson, and that made me unhappy because as Jennifer's father I feared for their safety. I always made a point to alternate my facial expressions—sad and angry—as I helplessly waved good-bye when they rumbled down the driveway and out into the street.

My little sweetheart had grown up. Each day I could see that her love for Sid was becoming stronger and deeper, until it was obvious that they would one day be husband and wife. That made me happy—as I could envision a wedding in the distant future. One eerie weekend when a strange weather pattern slithered across California's coastal plains, over the mountains and into the deserts, Jennifer and Sid drove to Las Vegas and got married. That made me very unhappy.

They decided not to tell me for a month. That did not improve my happiness factor. But they are building a good life together, and there are many events a father cannot control but must learn to support and encourage for the long-term good.

After a couple of years, and some gentle persuasion from his favorite father-in-law, Sid started teaching a small Bible study. That makes me very happy. However, the Bible study meets in a storefront in a seedy part of Santa Ana—my friends won't even drive through that area at night—so that does not make me happy. But Sid is faithful to the study, and I can expect a phone call from him every Friday afternoon as he labors to extract the truth from a passage of Scripture. And he loves a young woman whom I have loved her whole life. So again I am happy.

A few weeks ago a reporter from the *Los Angeles Times* called because she was interested in Sid's Bible study and was looking for a quote from me. She ran a feature article on Sid and included a large photograph of my daughter. Other papers across the country picked up the article and reprinted it or sent reporters to write their own stories. Even a reporter for a German magazine showed up to interview them. CBS came around with cameras rolling, as did the Channel 9 news team. Now all this interest in Sid's Bible study and the resulting addition of new members to the group made me very happy. The real reason the news media were interested in Sid, however, is because he is one of the few Christian tattoo artists, and the photograph of my daughter in the paper included a large portrait of Jesus on her back. Would you like to guess whether her having a tattoo makes me happy or unhappy?

Jennifer and Sid minister to others within the context of postmodern popular culture. But what exactly *is* today's culture? During modernity a split occurred between highbrow and lowbrow culture. High culture usually is associated with the arts: painting, sculpture, plays, classical music, poetry, and literature. Low culture is associated with entertainment: television, movies, popular music, commercial art, and potboiler novels.

For highbrow culture to be fully appreciated, a degree of education is required. Since high culture implies a degree of sophistication, it generally is seen as an elitist pursuit for the affluent and educated. Low culture, on the other hand, is popular culture. It is entertainment for the masses, requiring little in the way of previous knowledge or art appreciation. In fact, in the earlier part of the century silent movies (low culture) were used to help introduce new immigrants to American culture and values.

Today, low (or popular) culture is even more the culture of the majority in our society. Advances in communication technology have made it ubiquitous. Much of it is driven by economic interests, specifically, to provide the greatest number of consumers with commodities. Marketers have the challenge of making those commodities desirable to consumers. In other words, popular culture is all about commodification, commercialism, and consumerism.

Postmodernity also blurs the distinctions between high and low culture by offering reproductions of pop images as highbrow art—remember Andy Warhol's Campbell soup can?—and by the mass reproduction of high art. Furthermore, in postmodern culture the distinctions of high and low are irrelevant. Understanding a work of art no longer requires an expert critic or interpreter because one either despairs of understanding or finds one's own meaning. Either way, the object of art has done its job.

Some people, like art critic Hilton Kramer, regret the disintegration of the dividing line between popular and high culture. In their minds popular culture is something like a computer virus that insinuates itself into every nook of society, overwriting what is there with its own program, replicating itself, corrupting the existing files, and causing untold damage to the world of high culture. Some Christians, like Ken Myers, believe that high culture provides a more faithful means of conveying the truth of God than popular culture. Nevertheless, it is popular culture that we must address because it has engulfed our whole society.

The examples of postmodernism that we explored in chapter 3 may seem remote, academic, or unrelated to real life. After all, how many philosophers do you hear editorializing on all-news radio stations, writing scripts for soap operas, or analyzing the role and meaning of sport at a baseball game? The specialized vocabulary and lofty ideas of scholars are abundant in universities but rarely heard in ordinary conversation. Still, the literary and philosophical ideas of postmodernism have infiltrated popular culture and are influencing our social environment. More and more each day, how we think about ourselves, our communities, our nation, and our world is subtly transformed by the deep philosophical opinions that undergird our experience of life. Postmodernism has become the essence of popular culture—which means our children are exposed to it every time they turn on a television, read a schoolbook, or skim through a magazine.

In the last chapter we explored what postmodernity comes after. Let's revisit those themes and see how they are bubbling to the surface in popular culture. As the relevance of postmodernity to your everyday life becomes more evident, you will be able not only to brace yourself for the future but also to embrace the future with hope and vision.

After Rationalism

Frank is a Christian who practices his faith in a postmodern way. He rarely misses a weekend service or Thursday night Bible study in my church. He is a superior court judge, an advisor to our church board, and a devout Roman Catholic (don't ask). For anyone who is interested in deepening his prayer life and commitment to Jesus Christ, Frank teaches a course called "The Spiritual Exercises of Ignatius." Those participating make a yearlong commitment to an intensive course of spiritual discipline that includes an hour of prayer every morning. He also participates in Daniel's Inn, a group of Christian judges and attorneys who meet together for spiritual encouragement, guidance, and support.

Postmodern religion is eclectic. Believers pick and choose their favorite authors and teachers from among a variety of denominations (and non-denominations) and theological persuasions. Loyalty to the religious traditions of their parents and grandparents is not important to postmoderns. Since popular culture is no longer strapped by the constraints of neat, rational categories, postmoderns are free to celebrate a new openness to nonrational entities (angels) and experiences (miracles). Rather than dismiss the supernatural or spiritual experience out of hand, postmoderns want to know what we can learn from such things.

Unfortunately there are no boundaries to postmodern inquiry, and people are as likely to explore New Age quasi-spiritual technologies, occultism, and UFOs ("the truth is out there") as they are traditional religions—in fact, maybe more so. What is even more common is the lumping together of religious ideas from a variety of spiritual sources: Buddhism, Hinduism, Christianity, animism, near-death-experiences, and so on. This is not to say that postmodernists take these religious systems seriously. For instance, they don't view occultism as if it were directly related to dark or satanic forces. Instead they see it as a form of play. Postmodernity engages in lots of play: playing at love, at sport, at fashion, at psychotherapy, and so on. Rational criteria no longer control the interests (or meandering) of the human mind.

One result of this is a growing interest in mysticism. Protestants and Roman Catholics have seen a strong resurgence of the teachings and practices of Christian mystics—some Catholics even have delved into the beliefs and exercises of Zen Buddhism in their quest for spiritual experience. Modernity was not able to supply all the answers to satisfy our rational minds and our need for security and hope, so people are starved for experience. Intellectual propositions aimed at the brain cannot replace the passion for which the heart yearns. Modern lovers spent countless hours defining their love. Postmodern lovers spend their hours loving.[1]

As we have seen, the carefully constructed rational arguments of scholars, scientists, and apologists break down in postmodern discourse. Instead, the postmodernist looks to personal experience for proof—perhaps reminiscent of the premodern invitation "Come...and see" (John 1:39,46). In a postmodern culture, rational arguments against faith no longer carry the same weight. But on the other hand, neither do rational arguments in favor of faith, which means Christians may find their apologetics from the last two centuries to be less and less effective.

After Scientism

A national news service reviewed a report that appeared in *Nature* magazine. Researchers had found that a woman's attraction to a man's appearance varies through the month. "When a woman is ovulating, or ready to conceive, she is likely to prefer men with more masculine features," we are told. "The researchers believe this phenomenon is inborn...for sound biological reasons: In the animal kingdom, masculine looks denote virility, and thus the ability to produce healthy offspring."[2]

The article reported these findings in a lighthearted way, as though they were interesting but not to be taken seriously. The writer concludes: "The findings suggest at least one piece of practical dating advice: A man who gets rejected by a woman might have more success if he asks her out again in a week or two." In other words, scientific research, which sometimes looks frivolous to outsiders, becomes even more frivolous when it is put to use in such inane applications as increasing one's sexual attraction.

Postmodern culture generally treats science in a playful and ironic way, as opposed to the reverence science was shown in the modern era. Science, however, continues to take itself very seriously and, besides the church, is one of the staunchest holdouts for modernity in Western society. Some postmodernists resent scientism and the assumption that scientists alone have access to the truths of the universe through rational and empirical methods of research. They remind us that more than two-thirds of the world's population either do not know or do not accept science as having the last word.

Postmodernism is not a serious threat to scientism. Almost everyone working in the "hard" sciences tend to ridicule postmodern attacks on their worldview. They point out that postmodernists use the very methods they criticize when they argue against the roles of rationality and observation in science. But postmodernists are immune to charges of hypocrisy. To them, all of life and culture is hypocritical: There is no single, straightforward path.

Thirty years ago, when advertisers wanted to impress their audience with the potency of their product, they would dress an actor in a white lab coat and put him in a laboratory complete with beakers and microscopes. The word of the scientist was regarded as the most conclusive, most authoritative, and most reliable. Since that time movie stars and television celebrities have taken over the role of selling products. We no longer are sold on the word of scientists but of people we trust, that is, people whose faces we know and whose personae in movies or news broadcasts have created a sense of intimacy. Advertisers value the testimonials—or exhortations—of famous people, especially if their promises match the credibility of their perceived images.

Science can no longer stand alone in society as being able to justify its own existence. It has to stand for something—it has to "perform," according to Jean-François Lyotard. The scientist is no longer society's hero, leading us to a golden age of productivity, abundance, and happiness. In fact, there are depictions of scientists in culture (like Dr. Moreau) in which their regard for human life has been compromised by their obsession for discovery and control over biological forces. Likewise, the American Medical

Association often is perceived by health-food advocates as a large, oppressive institution with a vested interest in its own tradition that blocks and persecutes practitioners of nontraditional medicine and therapy.

In the minds of many people, science has been taken over by the government and industry. The government has a stake in science, both in the production of efficient killing machines and in providing controls over dangerous uses of technology, such as electronic crime and cloning. American industry, in creating a demand for new products and then finding ways to satisfy those consumer "needs," looks to its research and development departments or university labs for innovations on old products. These innovations make existing products obsolete in light of the "new and improved" item, or they create new products that the marketing departments then hype in a way that convinces people they cannot live without one. A lot of bioscience research is driven by the desires of consumers to perfect their physical appearance, resist aging, and produce flawless offspring.

People have high expectations for future scientific accomplishments—cures for cancer and AIDS, for instance. But these are not the optimistic expectations of a utopian future. Rather they are the demands that we place on science and for which we feel scientists are responsible. After all, was it not their technology that helped create new illnesses and threats to human health? And did not science promise to provide us with cures? And is it not also true that billions of dollars every year are lavished on scientific endeavors that should eventually produce something for the good of humankind?

After Historicism

In the movie *Bill and Ted's Excellent Adventure,* two high-school students who have fallen behind in their education must either present a history report to a school assembly or risk being failed. Through the benevolence of a future society that reveres their memory and is founded on Bill and Ted's personalities, they are able to time-travel to collect a variety of history-making heroes such as Socrates, Napoleon, and Abraham Lincoln. The movie makes no attempt to plumb the thinking or accomplishments of these historical figures—they are merely props, honored because they are well-known. The conclusion of Bill and Ted's history report has little to do with history. In a sense the movie seems to say that history can be fun but at the same time is pointless; nothing is taken seriously. The plot of the movie never leaves the immediacy of the present, and the theme never rises above the slogan "Party on!"

Popular culture does not think of history as the march of time, one event flowing out of another in a sequence or complete chain. Rather it views history as fragmented, as discrete events that have little relationship to one another. History, therefore, is useful as a potential source of entertainment, for highlighting political issues, and for recognizing the rights of minorities.

Movies and novels have performed a remarkable job of retelling (and rewriting) history, sometimes in quasi-documentaries, mixing factual details with fictional characters and interpretative plots.[3] The movie *JFK* combined film from the sixties with the dramatization Oliver Stone created in the nineties. *Forrest Gump* made use of computer technology to place a fictional character in film footage with President John Kennedy and even create a dialogue between them.

What is lost to postmodernity is the idea that history is going anywhere. Terry Eagleton, in *The Illusions of Postmodernism*, defines history as a "teleological affair" that depends "on the belief that the world is moving purposefully towards some predetermined goal." Nevertheless, he assures his readers that "There is no need to worry about how best to confront people who hold this belief, because there aren't any."[4] Thus, when we look back, we see a fragmented past with no immediate connection to the present and no bright outlook on the future. Popular culture retrieves items from the past for its own purposes; it makes use of relics and restores antiques, but does not actually venture into the past or appreciate history for its own sake.

Popular culture plays with history. A number of movies are almost impossible to place in any given time period. The movie *The Mask* is sometimes fifties- and sixties-ish and sometimes from the nineties. You cannot be certain. *Blade Runner* borrowed from the *noir* type of films (Bogart-style detective movies) of the forties but was set forty years in the future. Television characters such as *Hercules* are supposed to represent ancient history, but they use contemporary slang. Some movies even tinker with time and time-continuum paradoxes, either playfully, as in *Back to the Future,* or in a mind-boggling hyper-jump, as in *The Matrix.* Other movies incorporate so many flashbacks and flash-forwards that the confused audience gets lost in time.

In the past a central clue for fixing a movie in time was the use of period fashion, especially that of cars and clothing. Whereas some costume directors work hard at historic authenticity in a movie's wardrobe, there are contemporary movies in which clothing cannot be dated. This stems from the fact that popular fashion has become eclectic and some designers (and consumers) have adopted retro-fashion. Today, as opposed to twenty years ago, every style from every era works. Former uses of symbols to signify status are gone. Pricey athletic shoes are worn by street gangs and faded jeans are the uniform of the suburbs.

Through the 1980s and 1990s, clothing styles characteristic of punk, grunge, and gothic were used not only for group identity but also "to quote, invert and distort dominant meanings." According to Dick Hebdige, fashion is used to pursue postmodern goals, to "lay hints of disorder, of breakdown and category confusion: a desire not only to erode racial and gender boundaries but also to confuse chronological sequence by mixing up details from different periods."[5]

After Absolutism

Few would argue that the evidence points to widespread moral decline in our society. But the moral breakdown that Christians bemoan cannot be attributed to Hollywood, left-leaning media, or secular humanists. None of these institutions has the power to effect the moral changes that separate today from yesterday. Rather, morals have floundered because they are based on absolute truth, which few people still accept. Even people who claim to believe the Bible do not have the kind of trust in it that was fairly standard one hundred years ago.

Once absolutes are removed, we have a hard time answering the question "Why be moral?" which devolves into other questions, such as: "Why not have sex outside of marriage?" "Why not steal if no one will catch you?" "Why sacrifice your own freedom and pleasure to help others who are oppressed?" Popular culture can do no better than provide answers based in law, health, economics, or personal freedom. For a society that sees no future, those answers are simply not strong enough to overcome the urgency of the here and now.

Sometimes teenagers say, "People wrote the Bible. Why should I believe it?" If religion, like culture, is a human invention, then people who want to be religious must become "consumers of reality"—shoppers who weigh and compare the various claims of religions and determine what each one has to offer. But this sensibility in popular culture also makes consumers wise to the "realities" religious teachers try to foist on them.

Suppose a white-haired UFO-ologist comes to town with stories of alien abductions, elaborate conspiracies, and government cover-ups? The savvy shopper will recognize the human fingerprints on the infrastructure of his doctrine that suggest the activity of a busy, if not paranoid, mind. On the other hand, preachers who "construct realities"—that is, produce elaborate eschatological or systematic mental structures built from a collection of Bible verses—also will be treated with skepticism. Promises of a well-ordered and happy life based on biblical principles appear as dubious as electronic machines that measure one's spirituality. Even Job, the premodern hero of the Old Testament, knew there were no easy answers or simple formulas for life. Of course, people who surrender themselves to the belief systems of any group or subculture give their allegiance to the creeds of their founders, but almost everyone outside those subcultures sees their system as a postmodern form of idolatry. "[A] craftsman has made it; it is not God" (Hosea 8:6).

When advertisers attempt to launch new campaigns or a public-relations firm prepares to introduce its client to the masses, the controlling concern is not "What is true?" but "What is believable?" The truth of a product or public figure may be noble but not sell to a mass audience. A commodity may be so good that its benefits are unbelievable, or it may be so mediocre that it cannot arouse interest. So the people on Ad Alley go to work on it, dressing it up with believable yet exciting promises of its performance and value. But are these promises true?

As we have seen, postmodernity is characterized by a suspicion of meta-narratives. Therefore, whenever someone in popular culture makes statements that reflect absolute truth or universal values, the postmodern mind immediately wonders what he or she is trying to sell. Whatever image Madison Avenue is trying to promote, the street-smart postmodernist knows it has no direct relationship to reality, and he or she can therefore "see through the clunky attempts to manipulate our opinions and assets"—as Douglas Rushkoff so aptly put it. He goes on to describe the way Gen Xers react to television advertising: "When we watch commercials, we ignore the products and instead deconstruct the marketing techniques. That is what we love about TV. We have learned that 'content' means lies, and that in context lies brilliance."[6]

A number of recent television commercials poke fun at television commercials. Somehow they attempt to climb outside the screen and join the viewer as a companion and fellow analyzer of commercials, thus further confusing the notion of space between television and the audience and blurring the difference between reality and unreality. In postmodernity truth is either a spongy, changeable thing or it ceases to exist altogether.

In some ways, postmodernism can be seen as the triumph of cultural anthropology. After studying a variety of cultures, anthropologists announced that every society had its own mores and the customs and beliefs of one culture were as valid as any other. They somehow determined that no culture was any closer to the truth than any other. Walter Anderson observes, "The anthropologists probably deserve much of the credit—or the blame—for bringing out into clear view the remarkable range of realities that exist in a world that, one would have thought, had but a single reality."[7] Postmodernism adopted the outlook of the anthropologists and gave up any confidence of knowing truth.[8]

Does the fact of diversity between cultural worldviews prove the relativity of truth? That is a modern question but one worth asking. If five different cultures espouse five versions of truth, does that prove there is no truth? Or if we decide that each culture is "correct in its own context," does that really do justice to the issue? For perspective, we know that centuries ago most people in Western culture believed the earth was flat. But especially after Columbus discovered the New World, most people soon came to realize the world was round. Because one culture believed the world was flat and another, later culture believed it was round, can we say, "The world is both flat and round"? I don't think so. If worldviews differ between cultures, one culture may be closer to the truth than another; one may be correct and the other wrong. But that was not the conclusion that anthropologists had drawn, and my argument may be too rational to please postmodernists. Or maybe what we see is the triumph of Nietzsche, who asserted in *The Will to Power*, "There are many kinds of eyes. Even the sphinx has eyes—and consequently there are many kinds of 'truths,' and consequently there is no truth."[9]

After Realism

A few years ago, a friend of mine took his three sons to the Anaheim Pond so they could witness the filming of *Mighty Ducks 2* and be extras in the movie. Later he told me the stadium's empty seats were filled with life-size cardboard cutouts of people so that, on screen, the stands would look full. There are all kinds of camera tricks used to fool audiences. A viewer cannot tell the real people from the cardboard people. Of course, no one in a movie is real. Even the people who move and speak are only representations captured on film. Popular culture is populated with cardboard extras, jet pilots train in flight simulators, and people get sick in virtual reality rides.

But the gap between what is real and what is merely a representation doesn't end there. Along the Mediterranean coast, the impressive ruins of Caesarea protrude from the ground. A large stone plaque was discovered near the beautifully restored outdoor theater. This artifact is the only archeological evidence of Pontius Pilate's tenure as proconsul over Judea. Actually, the stone plaque on display is merely a replica of the original, which is kept in a British museum. But tourists still snap pictures of the replica to take home and show their friends the evidence of Pilate's governorship of Judea.

As a matter of fact, tourists are taken to many sites that could not possibly be authentic and other sites where authenticity cannot be determined for certain. When it comes to the "upper room," the Garden of Gethsemane, the place where Jesus delivered the Sermon on the Mount, the tomb of Lazarus, attempts to locate the exact locations are little more than educated guesses. In fact, Roman Catholics and Protestants each identify a different tomb from which they claim Christ rose from the dead. In other words, one does not tour the land of Jesus but a fantasy land, a place that has little concern for the "details"—such as whether the revered sites are authentic. After all, it is the experience that counts.

Someone may argue, "At least the Sea of Galilee is real!" Yes, but the boats skimming across its surface—supposed replicas of the disciples' fishing boats—are much larger than in ancient times (to accommodate all the tourists) and are driven by powerful diesel engines (the sails are merely ornamental). And consider the fact that entrepreneurs have laid a concrete structure barely beneath the rippling surface of the Galilee so pilgrims can simulate walking on water. Not only are they so far from the original as to totally lose it, they deface the site and demythologize the original event by reenacting it through the artifice of human technology. By walking on a wall that makes it look through a video camera as if they are walking on water, tourists actually perform a parody that calls Jesus' miracle into question. What happens when the tour is over? Everyone returns to the real world, and the land of the Bible is remembered like a trip to Disneyland.[10]

Since postmodernity is what comes after the universe no longer "really" exists, how does this rejection of realism show itself in popular culture? To answer that question, let's take a look at the entertainment media and the worlds of art, politics, and law.

The Collapse of Realism in Film

There is a remarkable line in the movie *E.T. the Extra-Terrestrial* that demonstrates how reality breaks down within the medium of film. The hero, a boy named Elliott, discovers an alien life form in his shed. Toward the end of the movie, he and a few of his brother's friends try to help E.T. rendezvous with his landing party so he can return home. At one point a boy named Greg says, "Well, can't he just beam up?" To this, Elliott gives the snide reply, "This is *reality*, Greg."

The reference to "beam up" plays on a well-known means of transportation in the *Star Trek* television series and movies. To beam people up means to transport them from a planet's surface to an orbiting spacecraft by transferring them as particles and reassembling them in a special chamber. Everyone in the *E.T.* story knows exactly what Greg means. The question is perfectly rational given the context of the movie and the nature of sci-fi films.

The odd part of this brief dialogue is the fact that up until that moment we were watching the movie *E.T.* the way we watch movies like *Star Trek*, which means we were willing to suspend judgment about what can and cannot happen because we know the story is fantasy. But Elliott's reference to reality suddenly throws him into the audience as one who knows the difference between *Star Trek* fiction and real-life nonfiction. In doing so, it makes the viewers lose their sense of boundaries; where does the movie leave off and reality begin? Does Elliott belong in the seat next to us or on the screen?

In making reference to other movies, *E.T.* enhanced the realism of its own plot, which had reached a critical and emotional climax. Nevertheless, *E.T.* was a total fiction! The foundational elements of *E.T.* were not real life but other movies—movies that had to do with spaceships, alien creatures, government intrusions into private lives, and so on. The myths that supported the *E.T.* plot were borrowed from other movies, yet they were myths so prevalent within culture that moviegoers bought the plot enough to shed tears over the dying puppet.

The Collapse of Realism in Television

Television also provides good examples of simulation. Edward Veith points out that instead of representations of the real world, we have "television programs about television programs, TV whose only content is television, such as the awards shows and talk shows."[11]

Television upsets our sense of reality in a multitude of ways. Ian Mitroff and Warren Bennis warn that television is "the primary testing ground for much of what we call reality. It is our central laboratory for the manufacture of unreality."[12] (They claim that television not only defines reality but obliterates the distinction between reality and unreality. Unreality "occurs when everything not only becomes a sub-branch of entertainment but does so in such ways that we are not even aware that it has occurred.")[13]

While many Christian leaders rant about the content of television programs (violence, sex, profanity), they miss some of the more important issues of how television has reshaped not merely our views on issues but our *view,* that is, the way we look at the world. There is something more dangerous about a technology that reshapes your thinking (even if you are watching something innocuous) than a technology that spews out trash. The trash is easy to turn off, but the medium itself is more subtle by far.

The Collapse of Realism in Art

A similar blurring of the boundary between reality and unreality is created in the surrealism of a painter like Salvador Dali and the fantasy art of a Boris Vallejo. Through his art Vallejo creates half-human, half-reptilian creatures that not only are lifelike but also are credible enough to be real. He brings forth creatures out of the fantasy of his imagination and onto the canvas, where they take on a real-life vividness. He explains that for the painting "to be successful, the scenes from your imagination must be convincing enough for a viewer to be willing to go along with you: to willingly suspend his disbelief and say, 'Yes, this could work.'"[14]

These words could be applied to a lot of the creation and redefinition of reality that goes on in popular culture. Make the fantastic look plausible, and society responds, "Yes, this could work."

The Collapse of Realism in Politics and Law

Politics represents another realm of popular culture in which we have witnessed a loss of reality. Such a strong skepticism hangs over the political process today that the term *politician* often is used derisively—someone who cannot be trusted, who will do anything, say anything in order to gain votes.

No doubt the encroachment of the media into the lives of political candidates has helped develop within them a greater concern for their physical appearance, especially on camera—and nowadays the camera is everywhere. Politicians are so concerned with projecting the right image that a new profession has been born: the spin doctors, whose job is to manipulate information and, if necessary, manufacture stories to cast the politician in the very best light.

Few people expect to receive an honest promise or admission from their candidates. Postmodern skepticism about what is real floods this public arena.

According to Walter Anderson, "We can also see an increasing theatricality of politics, in which events are scripted and stage-managed for mass consumption, and in which individuals and groups struggle for starring roles (or at least bit parts) in the dramas of life. This theatricality is a natural—and inevitable—feature of our time. This is what happens when a lot of people begin to understand that reality is a social construction."[15]

Postmodernism also has influenced the seemingly stable tradition of law by changing the way lawyers present their cases. For example, a renowned criminal attorney, Gerry Spence, published *How to Argue and Win Every Time,* a book that reveals the secret of his successful representation of clients who were condemned in the media and in the eyes of the public before they ever stood trial. His book is a powerful lesson in storytelling. He argues that a defense can become bogged down with logic, and that juries need to be made to *feel* the force of the attorney's argument. The case needs to be tangible, emotional, and dynamic. The best means for producing these effects is a well-crafted story.

John Grisham has done quite well as an author by writing stories about legal cases that include large helpings of human interest and passion. In his book *A Time to Kill,* a young attorney wins a controversial case with the use of a compelling story in his closing argument. It was the force of his story, not justice or law, that won over the hearts of the jurors. Good stories evoke feelings, and feelings have more influence than logic over human decision-making.

After Ethnocentrism

Heather Webb describes a Thanksgiving that she shared with a Muslim woman from Iran. As they ate, the woman expressed her sorrow and how much she missed her home and her culture's traditions. "She spoke of her family, with whom she had lived until she was married. In her home, she said, meals were a central part of their lives, a place where loved ones lingered for long hours, sharing the small events of the day, telling old stories (which only get better the fourth or fifth time around), and reveling in the consolations of friendship."

Professor Webb said, "I found myself longing for something that she had to offer, the opening of doors to another land, one I might never see nor be welcome to enter, yet one that elevates those very things that I yearn for.... As she spoke, I realized that our culture of instant gratification, convenience, and individualism was far more hostile to her way of life than I could have imagined."[16] And we might add, hostile to our own spiritual and cultural existence.

Popular culture in postmodernity is paradoxical. On the one hand, there is a strong movement to embrace pluralism (the acceptance of many faiths) and multiculturalism. On the other hand, each ethnic group and minority feel the need to exert their uniqueness and community's claims with ever greater force and, in some cases, defiance.

Postmodernism urges us to hear the voices of those who have grown up in cultures different from our own, since those voices express concerns that deserve to be heard and addressed. Yet some postmodern scholars claim it is impossible for one culture really to understand and communicate with another. When this is played out in real life, subcultures and minorities often despair of rational discourse, due process, and negotiation. They become less concerned with "justice for all" than with guaranteeing that their will is accomplished.

Popular culture responds to multiculturalism with enthusiasm and interest—but with the same consumer impulse and playfulness that marks its other pursuits. Some postmodernists pride themselves on their varied cultural experience, and a few have a genuine experience of other cultures. But the majority who think they know other cultures have done little more than sample them, as if tasting wines or nibbling a variety of cheeses. Generally we experience only a caricature of other cultures, from which we learn no more than we would from the Disneyland ride "It's a Small World."

Popular culture is a mishmash of national identities, a carnival of cultures, a gathering of the tribes. Wherever there is a community with a strong cultural flavor, we will descend on it with cameras in hand. Soon artifacts of that culture will be remanufactured and mass-produced (in plastic) so that culture-starved middle-class Americans can have a vicarious experience of another culture—as Paul Simon thrilled American audiences by borrowing African music to produce the *Graceland* concert. In the meantime, the ethnic culture that is being plundered is in danger of seduction by Western ways and commercialization.

Along with the collapse of highbrow and lowbrow culture into postmodern popular culture, another strange phenomenon has occurred. The music and movie industries have celebrated and popularized the clothing, language, and lifestyles of street gangs. Rap music, for example, exposes all classes of youth to values and themes that are common among gangs: vulgarity, violence, crime, anger toward police, and resentment toward society. Through music, gangstas provide a narrative of one aspect of life in the inner city, and with their videos they take us there. As a result, gang culture is no longer a lower-class affair. It now infiltrates all levels of society.

How has postmodernism been a factor in popularizing lower class behaviors and values? Two postmodern assumptions have turned the attention of popular culture toward the lower class: (1) "These people have been oppressed" and (2) "These people have retained a strong culture and cultural identity." The first assumption, "these people have been oppressed," asserts that ethnic minorities in America have been oppressed by the predominantly white society and that females have been oppressed by males. The civil-rights movement highlighted the oppressive nature of segregation and discrimination in education, employment, and even religion. Affirmative action legislation was an attempt to redress these wrongs, an admission of bad policy, and, in a way, a kind of national apology.

Postmodernism has given a lot of attention to the way institutions and society continue to favor traditional power structures and oppress those who live on the margins. Thus popular culture looks for ways to give marginalized groups a voice in society—to put them in front of the camera and let them tell their stories to the whole world.

Now for the second assumption: "These people have retained a strong culture and cultural identity." In the 1970s and 1980s, Jean Baudrillard retraced the steps of Alexis de Tocqueville across America, but what Baudrillard found was a desert, an empty nonculture. Sometimes our sense of nonculture (the lack of rites of passage, meaningful involvement in religious ceremonies, tight-knit community, and so on) makes us envy families that have retained strong ethnic ties within a well-defined culture.

After Objectivism

There is a poignant scene in the movie *City of Angels* that demonstrates postmodernity's attitude about feeling. Nicholas Cage plays the role of an angel who falls in love with a surgeon, played by Meg Ryan. He approaches her in a library, and their conversation quickly turns from literature to medicine, at which point he tells her, "You're a good doctor." She asks, "How do you know?" And he responds, "I have a feeling." The modern character (surgeon/scientist) is standing face to face with the postmodern character (an angel), and her response is predictable: "Pretty flimsy evidence."

At that point the angel performs a demonstration for her. He takes her hand and asks her to close her eyes. He then strokes her palm with his index finger and asks, "What am I doing?" To which she responds, "You're touching me." "Touch," he says. "How do you know?" And she answers, "Because I feel it." He then says, "You should trust that. You don't trust it enough."

In popular culture people will justify many of their behaviors, actions, and decisions on the basis of their feelings, attitude, and mental state at the time. We are not evolving into the logical Spock of *Star Trek* but the intuitive Agent Mulder from *The X-files*—or a hybrid: part Spock, part Mulder. The point is, knowledge is not exclusively tied to rational observation but may involve separate knowing, connected knowing, or a combination of the two. "Separate knowers learn through explicit formal instruction how to adopt a different lens—how, for example, to think like a sociologist. Connected knowers learn through empathy."[17] Postmodernists do not need the world to make sense as modernity required. Rather "there is a 'New Sensibility'…about life that is not based exclusively on rational credibility but also on imagination, analogy, and intuition."[18]

What this means for popular culture is that an individual's personal feelings carry as much weight in his or her thinking as a scientific experiment. Other people within postmodern culture will defend the rights of individuals to their own feelings and sense of truth. The facts are irrelevant if people feel strongly about an issue.

When in the movie *The Matrix* Neo wanted to learn the secret of the matrix, he was told, "You have to experience it to know it." This represents a significant shift from modernity, which suggested that one's subjective feelings were fallible and unreliable in discerning the truth. We will return to this postmodern reversal—that "believing is seeing"—in the next chapter. For now we will simply note that the distance science used to place between the researcher and the object or person being researched no longer exists in popular culture. If postmodernists want to know something, they want to know by personal experience as well as objective study.[19]

Entertainment, art, politics, fashion, education, literature—postmodernity has altered every facet of our culture. Popular culture is like a social parade, a one-way procession that carries along with it music, fashion, education, law, and whatever else exists in the context of human interactions. There is no way to avoid being part of this parade because it includes everyone in our society. When we get dressed in the morning, we either are a recognized member of some group within the parade or else an oddball. People who try to stand on the sidewalk and stay out of the parade appear weird and backward. They cannot become effective leaders or opinion makers for the rest of society.

The Next Step

Where do we go from here? Perhaps we can piece together a few relevant details.

Popular culture is becoming increasingly postmodern. This means Christians will be presented with new temptations, new hardships, and new opportunities. We will have to develop new strategies if we are to truly represent God in this postmodern context.

Popular culture is not evil. Christians sometimes are tempted to forget that there is no Christian culture, only human cultures. No nation, no matter how dark, has ever been abandoned by God. Rather he has left a testimony to himself in every culture (Acts 14:16-17). Therefore we do not have to hate popular culture or stand against it.

Jesus sends us into popular culture the way God sent Him into the world (Mark 16:15; John 20:21). As much as we wish we had "the wings of a dove" so we could "fly away and be at rest" from the darkness and confusion of our culture (Psalm 55:6), God has work for us to do and we cannot accomplish it living outside of culture.

Our job is not to condemn the world. God sent Jesus to earth so He could "save the world through him" (John 3:17). If Jesus had dedicated His ministry to condemning the world, He would not have been much of a Savior. And we will not be of much use to our culture if we cannot learn, like Paul, to "become all things to all men so that by all possible means" we might save some (1 Corinthians 9:22).

Knowing the contours and geography of postmodernism is invaluable. Becoming familiar with what we are up against, as well as knowing the best entry points, will increase the effectiveness of our work in the postmodern world. Christians who want to minister in this new era must become students of the culture.

We cannot choose the era into which we are born. Perhaps you wish you had lived during the time of Moses or Jesus or Martin Luther. God chose you for this time. This may not be the easiest era for Christians, but we do not have time to waste whining and complaining. If you run from popular culture, you will not live close enough to people to be able to introduce them to the Savior. And make no mistake, there are millions of people today who know they need saving and are longing for someone to help them. Postmodernism presents tremendous opportunities for Christian ministry.

Chapter 5

POSTMODERN FAITH

Again Jesus said, "Peace be with you!
As the Father has sent me, I am sending you."

JOHN 20:21

One odd quirk about the church of my youth was that women were not allowed to wear slacks. Though slacks for women were introduced in the thirties, they were not widely adopted until the war effort of the forties when more and more women went to work in the factories. Although it became acceptable in mainstream culture for women to wear slacks, Pentecostal and fundamentalist Christians were slow to accept this fashion. They cited an Old Testament prohibition: "The woman shall not wear that which pertaineth unto a man, neither shall a man put on a woman's garment: for all that do so are abomination unto the LORD thy God" (Deuteronomy 22:5, KJV).

Today, of course, churchgoing women frequently wear slacks—sometimes when they are going to church! This change in attitude points to a time-lag between mainstream culture and Christian subcultures; a lag of ten, twenty, forty, and sometimes, one hundred years. For example, folk music had been around for a while before churches allowed acoustic guitars to enter the sanctuary. This is typical of the way new musical instruments have been introduced into Christian worship. According to Donald Hustad, "Few 19th century churches would consider using a piano for its services—the piano was a secular instrument, and not suitable for sacred purposes!" But because song leader Charles Alexander used a piano in revival meetings, "that percussive, keyboard instrument was sanctified for church use, and it soon became accepted by evangelical congregations for worship in the local church."[1]

The situation has not improved with the advent of postmodernity. In *Virtual Faith,* Tom Beaudoin observes that members of his generation who had belonged to various religious traditions "waded into pools of agnosticism, apathy, or cynicism" because "churches seemed laughably out of touch; they had hopelessly droll music, antediluvian technology, retrograde social teaching, and hostile or indifferent attitudes toward popular culture."

There probably are good reasons why Christian subcultures should lag behind the mainstream culture. Some cultural changes and trends run counter to the teaching and commandments of Scripture. The legalization of adultery between consenting adults in California did not change its status as a sin according to the Bible, and the church has neither the power nor authority to alter or compromise what the Bible clearly teaches. Christians are wise to follow Paul's advice in 1 Thessalonians 5:21-22, "Test everything. Hold on to the good. Avoid every kind of evil."

The problem, however, is that many older Christians do not bother to test cultural inventions and innovations but dismiss them without a fair trial. The basis of their decision lies either in taste, old cultural norms, or an emotional attachment to "the way we've always done it." And older generations tend to mistrust the ability of the youth to discern right from wrong in these matters. Sometimes this caution is well founded, but other times the youth have much more refined sensitivities to right and wrong in their fashions, fads, and music than their parents' generation can imagine.

Typically, Christians do not feel safe with societal innovations in customs, music, and fashion until those things have become commonplace and universally accepted. The churches of my youth often seemed trapped in an earlier period of human history that the rest of the world had abandoned long before. Young people, especially, chafe at this.

Christians should not feel compelled to adopt the customs or forms of worship of other cultures or of previous generations if there is no biblical reason to do so. If members of one church choose a style of worship that is led by a rock-'n'-roll band, they should not be criticized by another congregation that sings to the accompaniment of an organ and choir. The New Testament allows believers a lot of latitude for their personal convictions regarding eating, drinking, and other customs (see Romans 14).

There is no biblical mandate for the church to make use of the musical forms of its host culture. But here is the point: A church that wants to provide worship in the *lingua franca* of mainstream culture, that is concerned with how intelligible it is to its host culture, will be interested in the current style, trends, and music of that culture. One part of the issue relates to the preferences of people who already are believers, while the other part of the issue has to do with the church's effectiveness in communicating with mainstream culture.

The people who will care the most about whether the church is up-to-date in its music will always be the youth. They do not have the same emotional or preferential investment in older cultural forms, and they are more concerned with how they, their church, and their faith appear to their non-Christian friends. Will the church's music reveal the relevance of our faith to people on the outside, or will it make us look like aliens?

Because cultures change with time, Christians need to find new ways to present the gospel. We also need to produce fresh interpretations and applications of Scripture that will speak to our changing culture. If all we do is cling to our old customs and biblical interpretations—as if they were as inspired as the Bible—then we will lose touch with the world.[2] Rather than give people the impression that God was for yesterday, I want to see Christians represent the truth: that the God who identified Himself as "I AM" is for today, tomorrow, and forever.

With the advent of postmodernity we have an opportunity to reenter public life as a force for good and with new vitality in our message. When we listen both to popular culture and the Bible for fresh interpretations that will fit the times in which we live, the light of our witness will not be hidden from the people who need to see it most (Matthew 5:14-16).

The Opportunity of Postmodernism

When I first heard about postmodernism, it seemed too academic and erudite to provide a realistic opportunity for Christian witness on a grand scale. But the more the ideas and values of postmodernity permeate society, the more sense it makes to dive in and reshape our preaching (not our message) and practice (not our values or God's commandments) to give Christian ministry currency in the emerging new world.

Will people in postmodernity come to faith in Christ in the same way people did during modernity? Well, some people will, but not very many. For example, modernity became infatuated with "natural laws"—which even inspired some theologians to produce a "natural theology." Writing in the spirit of the time, Montesquieu argued, "Laws are the necessary relations which derive from the nature of things, and in this sense, *all beings have their laws: the divinity has its laws*, the material world its laws...man has his laws"[3] (italics mine).

Note how Montesquieu's statement (i.e., even "the divinity has its laws") underlies the thinking expressed in the well-known evangelistic tract published by Campus Crusade for Christ *The Four Spiritual Laws:*

Just as there are physical laws that govern the physical universe, so are there spiritual laws which govern your relationship with God....

Law one...God loves you, and has a wonderful plan for your life.

Law two...Man is sinful and separated from God, thus he cannot know and experience God's love and plan for his life.

Law three...Jesus Christ is God's only provision for man's sin. Through him you can know and experience God's love and plan for your life.

Law four...We must individually receive Jesus Christ as Savior and Lord; then we can know and experience God's love and plan for our lives.[4]

Notice how the gospel is framed in "laws" that correspond to the natural order, like the "laws of physics." This was an effective way of appealing to the modern mind, which conceived of laws operating in every order of reality.

But that assumption no longer holds true in today's culture. The world today does not think of physical laws as existing in nature. The idea that the universe was a huge machine was popular during the industrial age, and by thinking of the cosmos in this way, as Allen Wheelis said, "We come to believe that laws of nature *exist* in nature, that they reside there, silent, invisible, and eventually *discovered* by man." The truth, however, is that natural laws were "*created* by man with nature sitting as model."[5]

The argument from physical laws to spiritual laws still may influence some people, but it won't be very compelling for the majority of Western society, and even less in other cultures of the world. Therefore, it is time to look for new expressions of Christian truth that are more compelling for our contemporary climate.

Seeds of Postmodern Faith

I have long hoped one day to belong to a Christian community that lives in "real time," fully interactive with its host culture. After I was exposed to the growing influence of postmodernism and the waning of modernity, I took up a study of postmodernity to find points of entry for an authentic Christian presence, influence, and lifestyle.

My main resource was—and always has been—the Bible. I was nurtured from infancy on the fact that Scripture is inspired, eternal, and relevant to every culture. I am convinced of the truth of Paul's statement that God "has not left himself without testimony" and has made plain to all nations "what may be known about God" (Acts 14:17; Romans 1:19). So even when others can envision only darkness on the postmodern horizon, I see God going before us, extending His love and light into the new world.

In working my way through the Bible one year, I was struck by a story in John's gospel that may provide the seed for planting faith in postmodern hearts. The most important event of Jesus' life on earth was His resurrection. As important as His teaching, His miracles, and even His crucifixion were, all of those things were useless and futile if Jesus was not raised from the dead (1 Corinthians 15:12-17). Not only does the resurrection complete and validate the rest of Jesus' ministry, but it also provides Christians with a dynamic spirituality because our hope and trust come through a life-transforming encounter with a living Savior.

The resurrection of Jesus Christ as the bedrock of Christian hope and theology is one thing, but *belief* in the resurrection of Jesus is something else.[6] Not everyone will be able to believe that Jesus rose from the dead when they first hear the story (see Acts 17:32). Nevertheless, people often find that over time the right kind of faith grows within their hearts so that they can believe.

In his story of Jesus, John describes the different ways that people reacted to the news of the Lord's resurrection. John shows that people can arrive at faith in at least three different ways. We will zoom in on the disciples' reactions to Jesus' resurrection and then see how those reactions relate to faith in Jesus Christ.

Faith That Comes Through Simplicity

> On the evening of that first day of the week, when the disciples were together, with the doors locked for fear of the Jews, Jesus came and stood among them and said, "Peace be with you!" After he said this, he showed them his hands and side. The disciples were overjoyed when they saw the Lord.
>
> Again Jesus said, "Peace be with you! As the Father has sent me, I am sending you." And with that he breathed on them and said, "Receive the Holy Spirit. If you forgive anyone his sins, they are forgiven; if you do not forgive them, they are not forgiven." (John 20:19-23)

This first response to Jesus' resurrection is a faith of simplicity: The disciples saw the risen Lord and believed. They took His resurrection at face value. They did not have metaphysical questions to put to Him, they did not ask to see His driver's license, they did not need proofs that the One who stood before them was truly Jesus Christ, risen from the dead. Their response was simple because it did not entail any of the complexities of philosophical or legal proof. Jesus rose, appeared to them, and they believed. This is a model of premodern religious experience.

Faith That Comes Through Skepticism

> Now Thomas (called Didymus), one of the Twelve, was not with the disciples when Jesus came. So the other disciples told him, "We have seen the Lord!"

> But he said to them, "Unless I see the nail marks in his
> hands and put my finger where the nails were, and put my hand
> into his side, I will not believe it."
>
> A week later his disciples were in the house again, and
> Thomas was with them. Though the doors were locked, Jesus
> came and stood among them and said, "Peace be with you!"
> Then he said to Thomas, "Put your finger here; see my hands.
> Reach out your hand and put it into my side. Stop doubting
> and believe."
>
> Thomas said to him, "My Lord and my God!" (John 20:
> 24-28)

Thomas responded to reports of Jesus' resurrection with skepticism. He made a commitment to doubt rather than faith when he said, "I will not believe it." Thomas required proof, reasons, physical evidence. He wanted Jesus to prove rationally and empirically that He was alive from the dead by allowing him to examine His wounds. Thomas played the scientist looking for evidence to prove the Resurrection hypothesis. His response parallels the modern era's reliance on reason and empirical proof.

Faith That Comes Through Symbols and Signs

> Then Jesus told him, "Because you have seen me, you have
> believed; blessed are those who have not seen and yet have
> believed."
>
> Jesus did many other miraculous signs in the presence of his
> disciples, which are not recorded in this book. But these are
> written that you may believe that Jesus is the Christ, the Son of
> God, and that by believing you may have life in his name. (John
> 20:29-31)

Jesus acknowledged Thomas's faith, but there is a hint of disappoint-
ment in His words. Jesus spoke of another kind of faith, one that is not
dependent on visible evidence, one that entrusts itself to Jesus on the basis
of the truth contained in the message of the Resurrection. People who are
capable of this kind of faith, according to Jesus, are "blessed." These people
are compelled by the story of Jesus. They do not need to "see" first and then
believe. They move from the story to an experience of the resurrected Jesus
without having all their doubts resolved or all their questions answered.
Most people, and especially moderns, do not find it easy to embrace this
kind of faith. But like "costly grace," there is a "costly faith." Cheap faith
requires no real risk, trust, or life-changing decision.[7]

Jesus paid special tribute to people whose firsthand experience is with
story rather than physical events. Therefore, their faith is "symbolic" (or
semiotic), in the sense that they are shown one thing (the story, or sign) that
represents something else (the event, the resurrection of Jesus). The story
stands for what actually happened in the life, ministry, death, and resurrection of Jesus Christ. These people believe through the symbol or sign to the
reality. This sequence of truth, story, and faith experience matches the postmodern worldview.[8]

Symbols and signs can be analyzed—as they have been, endlessly, in
modernity—but their real intention is to evoke the imagination of the
hearer. The same is true of Jesus' parables, and the result is not merely an
acknowledgment of truth but a discovery within the hearer who suddenly
experiences the meaning of the parable. Eugene Peterson has a lovely way of
explaining how the parables of Jesus worked:

> As people heard Jesus tell these stories, they saw at once that
> they weren't about God, so there was nothing in them threaten-
> ing their own sovereignty. They relaxed their defenses. They

walked away perplexed, wondering what they meant, the stories lodged in their imagination. And then, like a time bomb, they would explode in their unprotected hearts. An abyss opened up at their very feet. He *was* talking about God; they had been invaded!

…But the parable didn't do the work—it put the listener's imagination to work. Parables aren't illustrations that make things easier; they make things harder by requiring the exercise of our imaginations, which if we aren't careful becomes the exercise of our faith.[9]

Walter Brueggeman agrees with Peterson when he writes, "The work of preaching is an act of imagination, that is, an offer of an image through which perception, experience, and finally faith can be reorganized in alternative ways." He points to the work of French philosopher Paul Ricoeur, who held that imagination "is the capacity to work through images, metaphors, and narratives as a way of evoking, generating, and constructing an alternative world that lies beyond and in tension with the taken-for-granted, commonsense world of day-to-day experience."[10]

When people come to faith through symbols and signs, they do not necessarily sidestep or abandon the simplicity of the disciples' faith or the skepticism of Thomas's faith but rather add to them. In other words, no one can read John's story without going first through the disciples' simplicity and Thomas's skepticism. This gives the reader a choice that was not available to either the disciples or Thomas. Symbols and signs follow simplicity and skepticism, but they also go beyond them by resulting in an *experience* of the truth. Thomas began with personal experience and arrived at faith, but the people Jesus says are blessed move from faith to personal experience; and the experience is *life* in Jesus.

In the last verses of the chapter, John explains why he wrote the story of

Jesus, and why he chose to include the particular miracles he recorded. The purpose of his book is to help the reader come to faith and through faith to life. That is the experience of the symbolic response: from story (sign) to faith, from faith to life. And life, in the context of John's gospel, has a special quality: It is *eternal life* with God the Father (verse 31).

The apostle Paul said the ritual of the Lord's Supper can "proclaim" the story of Jesus' death. In fact, he suggests this is a major way that this message will be communicated "until he comes" (1 Corinthians 11:26). That means symbols can carry an experience of the truth at least as powerful as preaching. Rituals, parables, stories, and symbols are part of the life of Christian worship that engenders faith in the hearts of believers and plants seeds of faith in the hearts of nonbelievers.

The power of symbols to reveal God's truth had a life-changing impact on Rob Silva, a tattoo artist who works at my son-in-law's shop. Rob had loved the Jesus he learned about as a child, but he left the church in his teens. "I was not into the religion thing, the whole hypocritical thing," he says. Then, as a young adult he experimented with church again, but because he was "punk and pierced," the pastor recommended that he "tone it down." That was it; Rob decided he did not need church.

Then one day he noticed a tattoo his friend Tom Hosko was sporting. It was a dagger with a skull for a handle, encircled with thorns, three crosses, and a drop of blood on the point. "Hey, what's up with the skull and crosses, man?" Rob asked. "I thought you Christians weren't supposed to have tattoos."

Tom began to explain to Rob each symbol: the skull was Calvary, the thorns represented the suffering of Jesus strung up on a cross between two thieves, and the drop of blood symbolized the promise of eternal life. Tom laid out the whole gospel by explaining every detail of the tattoo image. He then asked Rob if he wanted to be "born again," and Rob prayed with him right there.

"Everyone today has a symbol for something," Rob says. "You identify yourself through symbols. Some people use the swastika, for others it's the anarchy sign, for others it's something else. Our culture speaks in pictures. For us it's the cross, the dove, the fish, the crown of thorns."

The Faith of Our Children

We have looked at the church's tendency to lag behind the times, the need for new approaches to ministry, and my discovery of (at least) three different ways that people can come to faith in Jesus. The next step is to understand the connection between the three examples of faith in John's gospel to Christian faith as it relates to premodernity, modernity, and postmodernity.

The way of simplicity corresponds to faith in the premodern age, when almost everyone already believed in God. They merely had to decide which god (or gods) they should embrace. Judaism spoke of the "Most High" God—the God of gods. Christianity proclaimed the hope of knowing the Most High God of the Old Testament through the revelation of his Son, Jesus Christ. So the program was rather simple: The disciples were sent into the world to "make disciples of all nations" (Matthew 28:19). Those people in other cultures who believed the preaching of the disciples would also become disciples.

How does this premodern faith-through-simplicity differ from the postmodern faith-through-symbols? Both approach faith through storytelling. The difference lies in the fact that premodern worldviews were fundamentally different from today's. Premoderns believed they were dealing directly with reality, that they could experience it through their senses and describe it in words. Postmoderns, however, have blurred the boundary between reality and fantasy. Premoderns believed in the world as it was given to them by their culture. Postmoderns believe their world is merely one of a number of possible worlds and that each culture constructs its own world. Premoderns often accepted a story at face value, believing it embodied a particular truth. Postmoderns distrust the intentions of authors and probe stories for personal and perhaps multiple meanings.[11]

The skeptical response of Thomas corresponds to faith in the modern age, in which everything is doubted, examined, and analyzed. The modern response to religious claims has been "Show me!" Christians were able to answer critics with biblical citations until fairly recent times. That is because there still was enough residual influence of Christianity within culture to make people respect the Bible as an authoritative book. In fact, even non-believers framed their arguments in biblical language and nuance—it had become the only language available to them. But as modernity rolled on, that residue disappeared and people began to ask, "How do you know the Bible is true?" and "Why should we believe the Bible?"

Christians learned that people really needed to know why the Bible was to be taken seriously. Modern theologians—that is, theologians who were the true children of modernity—subjected the Bible to scientific scrutiny and decided that it could not hold up under the light of reason. Conservatives, on the other hand, denounced modernism in theology and eventually produced counterarguments to liberal theology and rational apologetics in answer to modern challenges. But both liberals and conservatives were thoroughly modern in the ways they approached the debate. The modern age gave birth to new schools of biblical interpretation (hermeneutics) that attempted to help Christianity become more modern.[12]

Even the most conservative sector of the church was modern in its approach, according to George Marsden. In *Understanding Fundamentalism and Evangelicalism*, Marsden argues that it is incorrect "to think of fundamentalist thought as essentially premodern." He argues that its close links to Scottish Common Sense philosophy and its fascination with scientific modes of thinking set it squarely within modernity. Fundamentalism is especially suited for the technological sphere of modernity. Writes Marsden, "Fundamentalism fits this mentality because it is a form of Christianity with no loose ends, ambiguities, or historical developments."[13]

The symbolic response corresponds with postmodern faith. Postmodernists do not require every *t* to be crossed or *i* dotted. Not every claim needs to be proven scientifically or empirically. In fact, rational arguments sound suspicious to postmodernists. On the other hand, they are more than willing to explore spiritual belief systems that cannot be neatly analyzed and categorized but must be approached through intuition, ambiguity, symbols, and story.[14]

Postmodernity shares an affinity with Christian mysticism in that both of them resist attempts to understand spirituality through reductionism—the practice of breaking a subject down to small pieces and analyzing each of them. The modern attempt to find rational meanings for symbols, to interpret and codify them, is resisted and considered unnecessary. Instead, symbols are allowed to speak apart from a scientific-type analysis. Postmodernists prefer to observe the whole and see what "truth" might emerge. I found in Simone Weil's writings the most beautiful suggestion I have ever seen in trying to unlock a symbol, an approach that would work for postmodernists: "Method for understanding images, symbols, etc. Not to try to interpret them, but to look at them till the light suddenly dawns."[15]

Much of our daily experience consists of "images"—flashes of symbols, objects, and designs that either tell a story or represent a whole collection of ideas. Consider the Nike wing logo, which not only is a company trademark but also a symbol of superior athletic performance tied to the legend of a Greek goddess of victory. In a culture like ours, a central concern of Christian witness is to strategically scatter its own "images" (symbols, stories) of faith throughout our community.

Rereading the Bible

More and more Protestant Christians—and we are way behind the Roman Catholics on this score—are discovering a new, yet old way of reading the Bible: *lectio divina*. The "divine reading" is a simple method of listening to God speak through the Bible to your heart rather than your brain. In reading the Bible this way, students are taught to be responsive to impressions they receive while they are reading and meditating on a passage of Scripture. In Christian spirituality, divine reading is just one part of a threefold spiritual exercise (*lectio*, reading; *meditatio*, meditation; and *oratio*, prayer).

I doubt that the current interest in Christian spirituality is simply a fad. I believe it reflects a new hunger (or old hunger that has reemerged) that was ignored or at the very least minimized by modernity. Esther de Waal's *The Celtic Way of Prayer* is one of many books that offers spiritual expression in a variety of paths that have long been minimized or overlooked. Though every orthodox Christian professes faith in the Trinity—even if we also profess our inability to comprehend such a thought—Celtic spirituality actually celebrates the Trinity in the repetitious actions of everyday life.

"Here is a profound experience of God from a people who are deeply Trinitarian without any philosophical struggle about how that is to be expressed intellectually," writes de Waal. "Perhaps the legend of St. Patrick stooping down to pick up the shamrock in order to explain the Trinity is after all more significant than we might have thought. It is as though he were saying to those early Irish people: Your God is a God who is Three-in-One and this is the most natural and immediately accessible thing in the world!"

All around their lives the Celtic people found a three-ness in their world through which they celebrated the Trinity. "The day starts with three palmfuls of water splashed on the face in the name of the three members of the Trinity, and from then on the Trinity is never far away."

Three folds of the cloth, yet only one napkin is there,

Three joints in the finger, but still only one finger fair

Three leaves of the shamrock, yet no more than one sham-
>rock to wear,

Frost, snow-flakes and ice, all in water their origin share

Three Persons in God; to one God alone we make prayer.[16]

There is something so natural and appealing about this earthy, practical spirituality that I find myself wanting to adopt it in my daily routine. Of course, Celtic spirituality may not work for everyone. Many postmodernists may need to look for more of a techno-spiritual pathway that does not look for links with nature so much as fusions with the frenetic energy of microchips and circuit boards. People who live near the earth and nature rejoice in God as the "Maker of heaven and earth." Perhaps people who live near technology and concrete cities will rejoice in God as "Designer and Encoder of all things." Whether we have a spiritual life that thrives in the city or requires frequent engagements with nature may turn out to be a question of where we will find our most useful metaphors, symbols, and parables. I look forward to seeing many crosscurrents of different models of Christian spirituality.

Christians who are heirs of modernity may find themselves uncomfortable with a faith that does not require or even trust lengthy arguments for the legitimacy of Christian doctrines. We are comfortable with principles and propositions, and we know how to memorize Bible verses. But we are insecure when it comes to experience. We have been well trained to distrust our emotions, feelings, and experiences when it comes to matters of faith. We have been warned that feelings can be deceptive. But at the same time, have we been warned that logic and reason also can be deceptive? Postmodernists know that potential deception lies everywhere.

In giving testimonies of their conversions, many evangelical Christians make such a point to downplay any experiential element that it is almost cliché to hear someone say, "When I received Christ, there was no lightning or thunder, and no divine voice spoke to me." Likewise, in the previously mentioned tract published by Campus Crusade for Christ, there is a model for modern faith. The tract includes a train diagram of three train cars—an engine, coal car, and caboose—which are labeled "Fact" (the engine), "Faith" (the coal car), and "Feeling" (the caboose), teaching us: "the relationship between fact (God and His Word), faith (our trust in God and His Word), and feeling (the result of our faith and obedience) (John 14:21)." We are told that "the train will run with or without the caboose," and in bold letters we are warned "Do not depend upon feelings."[17]

This model, however, creates an unnecessary separation between "God's Word" and "our feelings." There is no question that the Bible is our authority, but is pure reason the only legitimate way we can experience the authority of the Bible? We may also ask, "How do we take the Bible into our hearts and minds in a life-transforming way?" We do not have to say that we either believe the Bible rationally or experience it emotionally (or spiritually). We can legitimately have it both ways. To say, however, that the "facts" always precede faith and feelings is misleading and lacks theological warrant.

We should ask whether it is true that "feelings" always result from "our faith and obedience"? And is it true (universally) that the facts of Scripture always precede faith? A large number of Christians have told me that the first time they entered a church they "felt" something (which later they were able to describe as God's love or the Holy Spirit). Their faith began before they ever heard the "facts," and it began with a feeling. It is also true that the Bible is just as likely to produce feelings that lead to faith as it is to evoke faith by reason of its inherent legitimacy and authority.

The methods and messages of evangelism that Christians have come to take for granted fit well into a modern culture but not into postmodern culture. What would happen if we began including experience as an element in the conversion process? First, we would make faith possible for postmod-ernists who are not swayed by rational arguments. Second, we would intro-duce a factor that is not under our control, and this places us in a condition of absolute dependence on God. Perhaps this is where we need to stand in order to see God work.

What would happen if we allowed people to "feel" what we cannot explain, to know with the heart and not just the brain? We would open the door of faith to a wider audience than if we continued to insist on a rational belief in the facts as the only legitimate starting point of Christian faith.

In John 20:29, Jesus pronounced a blessing on the third type of faith, the faith of those who believe without seeing. I believe postmodern Chris-tians are in a unique position to be eligible for that kind of faith. In fact, when Jesus said these words to Thomas, he was looking into the future, when reports of his life and ministry would be taken around the world. He was thinking about people like us.

If we are going to promote faith through symbols, signs, and stories, then we need to have a reliable, authoritative source. I have three sugges-tions, but before we get to them I want to take a ride down the river of time.

The River of Time

In trying to get a clear picture of this historic moment for the church, I came across a helpful illustration from Basil Mitchell in Diogenes Allen's book *Christian Belief in a Postmodern World.* The simple sketch shows a barge floating down a river that slowly winds through large stretches of ter-ritory.

Imagine it with me. The river represents the flow of time through three ages of history: premodern, modern, and postmodern. The church is the barge floating on the river, carried forward in time. But as the barge entered the modern era, a couple of shoals threatened its safety. Those shoals, shown mid-river in Mitchell's illustration and labeled "Hume" and "Kant," are "the works of David Hume and Immanuel Kant which enshrine some of the most serious intellectual barriers to Christian belief in modern times."[18]

When the church (the barge) met these dangers, it responded in two different ways. According to Allen, "[T]heologians have either jettisoned some of their cargo (Christian claims) to lighten the barge and sail safely over them, or they have swung sharply to the other bank to remain premodern. That is, they have either become modern by getting rid of lots of traditional Christian claims, sometimes even the claims that God is Creator and Redeemer in Christ, or they retain the language of traditional Christianity but at the price of repudiating in various degrees the need to take into account knowledge from any other domain. For those who remain premodern, Christian doctrines can be affirmed and discussed as if Hume's and Kant's objections simply do not exist."[19]

I suppose many Christians of premodernity were hoping they could wait out the crisis of the shoals on the bank of the river. Of course, that meant they were no longer moving, and that is one reason why Christianity lost its influence, prominence, and importance in modern times. As Leonard Sweet has observed, "Christians are like everyone else—more inclined to clutch old maps than to sail on toward new continents."[20]

When the mass of conservative Christian scholars and theologians could no longer remain on the banks of the river and were swept into the modern age, they found a number of questions they had to begin answering. For the first time in history, they had to defend their existence. In the words of Walter Anderson, "Some people really believed that the modern era was going to bring an end to religion, the final triumph of reason over superstition: God is dead, remember?"[21] The intellectual climate was chilling toward Christian belief and warming for science, skepticism, and rationalism.

Coming late into modernity, Christians had to scramble to catch up with the intellectuals in order to present a solid defense against the philosophical and scientific attack of modernism. At the same time, there still were Christians who sought to avoid the whole mess by living in the simple, innocent bliss of premodernity.

But where has the river of time taken us now? For one thing, we are beyond Hume and Kant. We live in a different world than the one defined by Hume's skepticism and Kant's autonomous self. According to Diogenes Allen,

> The way forward is forward. The principles of the modern mentality enshrined in Hume and Kant do not form an impassable barrier which we either must accept or avoid. The actual situation is that the barrier they and others formed has collapsed. Theologians no longer need to labor within the tight, asphyxiating little world of the Enlightenment or to become premodern. But those who continue to jettison Christian doctrines to float the remaining cargo over the shallow waters of modern intellectual culture and those who continue to avoid modern intellectual culture do not realize this. They allow the thought of the modern world to determine the course to be followed by Christian theology. They remain prisoners of the modern mentality.[22]

With this incredible opportunity before us, Allen sees Christians on a barge that is hesitant to move forward again. We finally have developed arguments that work really well in the modern age and that makes us feel comfortable among moderns. So some of our religious institutions already are showing signs of entrenchment, preparing to defend themselves against postmodernity. But all they can effectively accomplish through resistance is to linger in modernity the way earlier Christians lingered in premodernity, and as we have seen, this results in devastating losses for the church in society.

Some Christians are going to fight for the preservation of modernity as if they are battling to defend orthodoxy. They will fight for Enlightenment values as if they were sacred. We may have to remind ourselves that the Enlightenment signaled a shift away from faith in God to faith in human reason. Postmodernism, on the other hand, says there is no basis for privileging reason over faith in this way.

Fundamentalist Christians—and probably fundamentalists of any other religion—will still prefer premodernity. Evangelicals have become comfortable in modernity, and so have liberals. So who among Christians will move forward into postmodernity? The church stands to lose ground again in postmodernity as we did in modernity unless there are Christians who see and accept the challenge to go forward. Otherwise, we will continue to answer questions no one is asking, continue to be up to date on all the old news, continue to have well-reasoned arguments among ourselves that no one else cares to hear.

Do we have to abandon every structure and rational system we built in modernity? And do we have to abandon the richness of liturgy and theology of premodernity? Definitely not. Christian faith that comes through symbolism, sign, and story could not come except through the simple (premodern) and skeptical (modern) stages of faith. The river of time continues to carry the past in its current, accentuating its relevancies as well as its discontinuities to the present. Ted Peters rightly observes, "One of the curious things about history is that it seldom really leaves anything behind. It accumulates. The premodern way of thinking has not been totally abandoned. It is still with us and continues to exist side by side with the more recent innovations."

He then suggests "another way to look at this matter. It may be helpful not only to think of these three phases as different chapters in the story of Western civilization, but also as chapters of one's life story."[23] In other words, Christian growth often begins with the most basic and simple notions of God (especially if one comes to faith as a child). But the believer eventually hits a skeptical phase when it is not enough to believe everything just because it was told to you by a parent, minister, or Sunday-school teacher. Still, if we persevere in our faith, we will come to a place of peaceful acceptance where we are able to rest in our belief without needing visible proof.

If we do adopt this paradigm, it is important that we avoid using it to evaluate other people or locate ourselves at a higher level of spiritual development. In fact, we probably cannot fully leave one level for the next. Peters suggests that "the three stages are not intended to establish a hierarchy, so that one would necessarily be motivated to leave one level completely to go and live at the next. I suspect that it is possible for a person of faith to live simultaneously at all three levels."[24]

Reconstructing the Faith

What materials do we need to construct a postmodern faith? Besides the *message* of premodern faith, and the *reasons* of modern faith, we need to supply the right *signs or symbols* for a postmodern faith. These symbols must lead to an authentic experience of God and His truth. As Jesus said to Thomas, "Blessed are those who have not seen and yet have believed" (John 20:29).

Postmodernity has adopted the research of modern anthropologists and linguists, who determined that what people can and cannot see is largely determined by what they are prepared to see. "Perception," according to Charles Tart, can be "distorted by the perceiver's training and needs." One overused example is that "Eskimos have been trained to distinguish seven or more kinds of snow." I have heard as many as sixteen! "We do not see these different kinds of snow, even though they exist, for we do not need to make these distinctions. To us it is all snow."[25] The argument is, you first have to believe there are seven different kinds of snow before you can begin to see them.

Walter Anderson observes, "People used to say, 'If I hadn't seen it, I never would have believed it.' The postmod switcheroo, which you hear often these days, is "If I hadn't believed it, I never would have seen it."[26] Such slogans reveal postmodern consciousness at work and sometimes at play. Many postmodernists appear to feel free to play around with symbols, verbal and visual. Jesus' statement to Thomas does not seem so outrageous in this context.

Postmodern faith is a "believing without seeing" that results in seeing. In 1 Peter 1:8 we are told, "Though you have not seen him [Jesus Christ], you love him; and even though you do not see him now, you believe in him and are filled with an inexpressible and glorious joy." This is the goal of postmodern faith, to nurture belief in the unseen in such a way that it leads to an experience of love for God and inexpressible joy. It is our love for God that motivates us to do His will. We are not motivated to conform our lives to His will on the basis of knowledge alone. Bare knowledge does not change people. (How many smokers know that cigarettes are likely to kill them?)

What is the key to believing without seeing? Symbols. Symbols are to the Christian what a white cane is to a blind person. A mustard seed, a bit of leaven, a fishing net, seeds thrown on four different types of soil—all of these are symbols to help us believe in the invisible kingdom of God. Interestingly, each of these symbols was supplied to us by Christ in His teaching.

Today, we have at our disposal four sources of symbols, signs, and stories. These sources are the sacred text of the Bible, spiritual community, rituals and sacraments, and our own experience of God in Christ. As we seek to connect with postmodernists who don't yet know God, we can draw from all four sources.

First, we draw from the sacred text, the Bible. Postmodernism celebrates the fact that every culture or tribe has its own sacred text, so we do not need an excuse for our use of the Bible. But for the Bible to provide fresh symbols that are meaningful to the postmodern mind, we must try to look at it differently. A lot of Bible study in modernity was bent on finding doctrines that could be set in a systematic framework. Postmodernists can hardly think of doctrines except as something constructed by humans, an artificial barrier to fence some people in and other people out.

With that in mind, let's use the word *doctrine* less and start substituting the word *teachings*. The latter is easier for postmodernists to accept in reference to inspired writings. The Greek word translated as *doctrine* (*didache*) is the same word the New Testament translates as *teaching*.

Doctrine refers to a body of beliefs forged by other humans in a previous era. Teaching is an activity that goes on whenever we read and reflect on the Bible. Doctrine is self-contained and static. Teaching, like the Bible itself, is alive—a dynamic event in which the truths of Scripture are examined and applied to real-life situations. We do not need doctrines in order to reveal Jesus to our world so much as we need beliefs that live, that can guide us through our everyday life, and that bring us back into contact with God.

Even though we may study and analyze the Bible according to our modern scientific criteria, the text must be allowed to speak for itself. And equally important, our use of the sacred text must also allow the Holy Spirit to work in the postmodern era just as he has been at work in all periods of human history.

The second source of needed symbols for postmodernists is a spiritual community, namely, the church. The church as the "body of Christ" (Romans 12; 1 Corinthians 12; Ephesians 4), a flock (John 10), a building (Ephesians 2; 1 Peter 2), and a bride (Ephesians 5; Revelation 19-20) is rich in symbols and stories. The church is also the repository of the ultimate story, the gospel. Through interactions with other members of the church, images appear that reveal God's love among His people, the healing nature of Christ, the presence of grace, and the power of the Holy Spirit.

One caution, however. The church must distinguish itself from the many cults that will continue to flourish in the coming years. There must never be any coercion to join a church or to stay in a church. Like the human body, there must always be an equal appreciation for all the members of the church—the stronger caring for the needs of the weaker. And we must be wary of religious movements that form around the charisma of one particular leader.

A third source for symbols to inspire Christian faith lies in our rituals and sacraments. We need to revitalize Christian rituals and find fresh applications of their timeless truths. Rituals are the closest thing we have to a purely symbolic worship and expression of our encounter with God, so they are essential for postmodern faith. Our rituals can proclaim the truth about Jesus through objects, signs, and movement (1 Corinthians 11:26). Also, our rituals possess the important quality of belonging to a sacred realm, which speaks strongly to postmodern yearnings for meaningful experience.

Some Christian communities may choose to adopt new rituals or to borrow rituals from other traditions. This may be a good trend providing no one attempts to make any local ritual normative for all Christians. Also, we must constantly monitor ourselves to guard against putting our faith in the ritual. Rituals are one domain of faith that constantly pose the danger of idolatry.

The fourth source of symbol and story is our own experience of God in Jesus Christ. We will be like the demoniac—and the symbols here are suggestive—who begged Jesus to let him join the disciples. Jesus, however, refused his request and instead sent him on a mission. Jesus told him, "Go home to your family and tell them how much the Lord has done for you, and how he has had mercy on you" (Mark 5:19). I can picture the man's face brightening with realization, as if to say, "I'm on it, Lord. I know exactly what to do!" Then he went, not only to his own home, but through all of the ten Roman cities east of the Jordan River.

We have our personal stories, forged in the crucible of our own walk with God. People who are longing for change are eager listeners when it comes to "testimonials." Only be careful not to sound too polished or rehearsed. Postmodernists have seen all the tricks the media use to sell, spin, and hype. What postmodernists look for is the people who speak out of their heart, unrehearsed and sincere.

Let the Symbols Speak

Before we can communicate through story and symbol, we must first learn to listen to symbols for ourselves. There is a way of allowing our minds to settle into the Bible, not to dissect, analyze, compare, and conclude, but simply to *be* with God's Word, and to be with the characters we come across or the truths we find.

I will offer one suggestion as a useful approach to reading the Bible in this way: Place your trust in the message of the text. According to Ted Peters, "The key to a postmodern hermeneutic is surrender. We need to surrender ourselves to the symbols so that they can lead us into their world of meaning. We need to listen, to follow. To do this, we must trust."[27]

God is constantly calling us to trust Him. Almost every lesson in the Bible, as well as every commandment, hinges on trust. When you come across something in the Bible that is not immediately clear to you, think of it symbolically. Then listen to the symbol. Rather than tear it apart, looking for its meaning, wait to see what sort of experience it yields. Postmodern faith can be a faith that leads to an experience of the living Christ.

Chapter 6

THE CHURCH AND THE POSTMODERN BAZAAR

Then Jesus said to his disciples, "If anyone would come after me,
he must deny himself and take up his cross and follow me."

MATTHEW 16:24

It was the early 1970s, and change was in the air. The antiestablishment sentiments of the sixties had reached the Christian community, and laypeople as well as theologians were talking about the need for new models and structures for the church. There were even some experimental congregations around North America that attempted to recreate the communal church found in the book of Acts.

In one congregation, a well-known Christian author and speaker took the pulpit to deliver his perceptive insights into the biblical nature of the church. He stood, half-hidden, behind the wooden pulpit, opened his larger-than-life Bible, and began to take his listeners on an intellectual journey into the heart of the issue, outlining God's intent for the church. When he came to what he felt was one of the most important points of his sermon, he gave his words as much force as possible. "The church is not an organization," he announced, "it is an orgasm."

A shudder went through the congregation, the speaker being the only one who was unaware of his blunder. His wife's face blanched, and she implored him with her eyes to look her way so she could give him some kind of signal. But it was too late. Certain that he had struck a chord with his profound insight, he repeated himself: "The church is not an organization, it is an orgasm." Then, when the people could no longer suppress their laughter, he realized his mistake, "Uh, I mean an organism."

The modern church was constantly creating "binary opposites," either/or choices: either an organization or an organism, either rational or emotional, either material or spiritual, either conservative or liberal. The postmodern church, in contrast, does not find itself in the same polarization as the modern church. The postmodern church is not bound by the same binary thinking that forces one to choose between modes of being or methods of operating.

The church of the modern era was infiltrated by its culture and led to believe there were rational, scientific methods for designing, organizing, and running a church. These were the same principles, in many cases, that applied to running a successful corporation. It also was believed that, with minor adjustments, these methods could be applied universally, that they would work in any context or culture. Simply refine the method according to rational and biblical principles, and any church would flourish.

I remember hearing a minister one time comparing his denomination to the McDonald's restaurant chain. He argued that people go into McDonald's because they expect to get a Big Mac, and people going to churches in his denomination should expect the same thing in every church. But the fact is, not all churches are the same, nor should they be based on the same model. Not all churches have access to the same resources, are located in the same socioeconomic environment, or have staffs with the same level of competency. To rubber stamp one church model over the entire globe is a mistake of modernity.

Churches are similar to, but at the same time quite unlike, corporations.

How you gauge the health of a living organism is very different from the measurement of the health of a successful corporation. All the corporation needs to do is produce a profit, hence the business axiom: "A large bottom-line profit covers a multitude of sins." As long as the company is in the black, many mistakes can be made. But an organism requires internal integrity to ensure that its organs are healthy.

Since not all churches are alike, in postmodernity we should not look for one, single, best church arrangement. Instead we need to adopt a flexibility that is characteristic of all living organisms. A church in any culture simply needs to be what the church is supposed to be in every culture: People should be able to point to the local church and say, "Now that's what Christianity should look like."

Contrast that with theological educator Simon Chan's belief that Western Christianity has exerted a harmful influence on the church in Asia. "Churches planted by denominational mission agencies simply reproduce after their kind and thus perpetuate [overseas] the deep divisions [found] in Western Protestantism," he says. "Their presence continues to be a major stumbling block to Christian witness in Asia." He also believes nondenominational agencies foster an even more serious defect, producing churches "without any sense of history or tradition."[1]

These concerns are, of course, postmodern. According to postmodernity, Western imperialism in the form of missions "marginalized" Asian cultures even as it invaded them with the intent to evangelize. Now that Western "hegemony" is universally under attack, the suppressed (or oppressed) voices of other cultures finally are being heard, and for Chan, those voices need to be heard in theology as well as in other disciplines.

Our churches need to be responsive to their respective environments, representing the life of God and the life of the spiritual community in a way that is comprehensible to the culture around it. Churches that have a strong commitment to preserve the past may not have the needed flexibility to make themselves heard and understood. Institutions that enshrine the past are not churches but museums.

Putting the "Cross" in Cross-Culture

Some time ago John Stott wrote a commentary on the Sermon on the Mount with the provocative title *Christian Counter-Culture.* According to Stott, everything Jesus taught in His sermon runs counter to the values of our culture. As Walter Brueggeman explains, living in a society where the reality of God is constantly denied requires Christians "to see about alternative practices, disciplines, and intentions that may sustain an alternative, subversive, countercultural identity."[2] But I would add that the church also is a "cross-culture," especially in two areas: Christians are called to cross into cultures other than their own with the gospel, and we proclaim a message that is shaped by the cross of Christ.

First, as we cross into other cultures with the gospel, we must accept the context and language of those cultures in order to effectively present the message of salvation. This means we do not live in secluded isolation from the world. Instead we find that in the world "we do not have an enduring city" (Hebrews 13:14), nor do we have an enduring Christian culture, but we are "aliens and strangers on earth" (Hebrews 11:13). In the catch phrase of Stanley Hauerwas, we are "resident aliens."

Second, the church is a cross-culture because the outlook, values, and beliefs of its members are shaped by the cross of Jesus Christ. Jesus taught that His servants would have to follow Him into death (John 12:23-26). He also made it clear that the disciple must constantly "take up his cross and follow me" (Matthew 16:24).

The cross of Jesus reveals the dynamic possibilities of cross-cultural ministry in two ways, expressed in the theological terms *kenosis* and *incar-*

nation. These terms also apply to our effectiveness in the various cultures where the church is present.

The *kenosis* is the self-emptying of Jesus that Paul beautifully described in Philippians 2 (perhaps quoting an early Christian hymn).

> Who, being in very nature God,
>> did not consider equality with God something to be
>>> grasped,
>> but made himself nothing,
>>> taking the very nature of a servant,
>>> being made in human likeness.
>> And being found in appearance as a man,
>>> he humbled himself
>>> and became obedient to death—
>>>> even death on a cross! (Philippians 2:6-8)

The words "made himself nothing" translate the Greek word *kenoo,* "to empty, make void." Paul uses Jesus' self-emptying as an example of humility for believers. If we are going to be effective in cross-cultural ministry—even if it is nothing more than talking to our next-door neighbor—we have to empty ourselves of the contents of our culture, its prejudices, conceit, and judgments.

Kenosis is leaving our own country—our culture, preferences, and security—as God called Abraham to leave his country to follow in complete obedience and dependence (Genesis 12:1; Hebrews 11:8-10). Paul also left his home to travel the world, becoming "all things to all men so that by all possible means I might save some" (1 Corinthians 9:22).

Kenosis also is "giving," and the postmodern church will reveal the heart of God toward the world through its generosity to nations, races, classes, and individuals who don't enjoy the wealth and luxury of the developed nations. Postmodernists will be less willing to invest in institutions such as organized religion and more willing to fund relief projects for victims of catastrophes, epidemics, mental illness, poverty, and homelessness.

The second theological term, *incarnation,* is not specifically mentioned in the Philippians text but is implied in verse 8, which says that Jesus was "found in appearance as a man." John gives one of the clearest descriptions of the Incarnation when he says, "The Word became flesh and made his dwelling among us" (John 1:14). In becoming human, Jesus stepped into the human predicament. He embraced human culture and spoke a human language. He also embraced our suffering, grief, sin, and guilt. He emptied himself of his divine prerogatives to unite with us in our lost condition so that he could bring us to God (Hebrews 2:14).

Kenosis and *incarnation* define the cross-cultural role of Christians in the world. The cross is the symbol of our self-emptying so we can move into other cultures without prejudice or casting judgment on them. The cross also is the symbol of the flesh-and-blood existence that we give to the gospel by actually becoming living witnesses in other cultures.

If *kenosis* and *incarnation* reveal the cross-cultural presence of the church in human cultures, then it is wrong to think of the church as being at war with cultures. The military metaphor of "culture wars" is not only unproductive for Christian witness, but it is altogether misleading. It is reminiscent of earlier eras of church history when so-called Christian nations went to war with pagan nations to force their conversion. Culture war is a poor term to describe how we are to relate to the non-Christian communities in which we live.

True, there are aspects of our culture—of every culture—that we would like to see changed. But cultural change rarely occurs through direct confrontation, and at the very least, that was not the method used by Christ. The culture-wars mind-set creates barricades, whereas the cross-culture approach builds bridges. Culture wars makes non-Christians our enemies, while cross-culture makes them our mission. Culture wars sets us outside of culture in opposition to it, but cross-culture puts us right in the heart of our culture as salt, light, and ambassadors of God.

Culture is very much like language when it comes to communicating the gospel. Though a language may contain many offensive and blasphemous words, the solution is not to replace it with another language. Until the coming of Christ, there is no one, perfectly Christian culture, nor is there any one, purely evil culture. Culture is not the enemy in our spiritual warfare.

Theology professor Ray Anderson is correct when he says, "The power struggle is not between the gospel and culture, but between the gospel and the 'powers' within any culture that dehumanize and enslave persons. Paul sought the renewal of the social structures and the humanization of culture, not the replacing of these structures and culture with a kind of freedom that destroys them."[3]

There are biblical models for transforming culture that Christians can adopt if that is what God asks of them. But our first objective is to present a witness within culture in which people perceive God's love and salvation. To be effective in postmodernity, we must not line up with the angry preachers who constantly engage in battles with the media, politicians, scholars, the entertainment industry, or anyone else who does not look quite right to them.

Jesus was engaged in cross-cultural ministry when "the tax collectors and 'sinners' were all gathering around to hear him" (Luke 15:1). However, not everyone was happy with Jesus' missionary zeal. The "Pharisees and the teachers of the law muttered, 'This man welcomes sinners and eats with them'" (verse 2). The Pharisees generally are portrayed as the bad guys of the New Testament, but it is only our poor eyesight that keeps us from seeing how much we are like them. Anyone who welcomes sinners and spends a lot of time eating with them, or in other ways relating to society's lowlifes, runs the risk of being misunderstood and maligned by other believers.

Christians always will have a missionary role to play in the world. The reason I bring up our missionary task is to remind you of the reason why we are interested in postmodernism. To be effective in postmodernity, we need to know its terrain, customs, and values. We need to study postmodernism the same way missionaries immerse themselves in a foreign culture in order to effectively communicate the gospel.

The Attraction of Opposites

Postmodernism arose as a reaction to modernism, and like all reactionary movements, postmodernism tends to go too far. In developing an idea of what the church needs to be in postmodernity, we can neither fully embrace nor fully dismiss postmodernism. But there is great value in selectively adopting those aspects of postmodernism that prove most useful to Christian ministry. Almost everyone in popular culture will alternately accept and reject elements of postmodernism. For example, we will likely see a wider use of nontraditional healthcare treatments (herbs, acupuncture), but people also will continue to seek conventional medical care.

The postmodern church will find a way to embrace oppositional ideals. In other words, if modernity made one claim, and postmodernity is claiming its opposite, we may need to find a way to alternate between the two, to discover how the church is sometimes an organization and sometimes an organism. Real life is not as neat as the either/or categories we tend to concoct, but more often includes both/and situations. We are not looking for a synthesis of the opposites or a virtuous mean between two extremes. Instead we are looking for the wisdom to be able to alternate between two valid but opposing ideals, at one time embracing one, and at another time embracing the other.

In his book *The Dismemberment of Orpheus: Towards a Postmodern Literature,* Ihab Hassan created what has become a famous list of contrasting styles by which he illustrates postmodernism's reaction to modernism.[4] Here are some of his contrasting pairings:

Modernism	Postmodernism
Purpose	Play
Design	Chance
Hierarchy	Anarchy
Distance	Participation
Centering	Dispersal
Root/depth	Rhizome/surface
Paranoia	Schizophrenia

Looking at Hassan's list of contrasting styles, we can detect a bias in favor of postmodernism. But the idea I find more compelling is that postmodernity has not yet been able to make such a discrete break from modernity and will likely continue to waffle between both columns.

For our purposes, I have composed my own pairings of binary opposites that can help give shape to new ministry initiatives in postmodernity. The value of such is that it reveals our complete dependence on Scripture and the Spirit of God for wisdom to guide us on our journey.

Community and Individuality

Many contemporary theologians have become enamored with the notion of community, and it appears in a variety of places as a panacea for all our ills. This is in part a reaction to the rugged individualism of modernity. Nevertheless, the spiritual value of solitude, the importance of the integrity of a single unit, and the unique gift of each believer all need to be preserved in postmodernity.

Postmodernity will not so much favor community over individuality (or vice versa) as it will redefine what it means to belong to a group or to stand alone. The Internet will continue to be a place where people experience greater interactions with others and greater isolation at the same time. The church needs to create space for both interdependence and independence, perhaps at last giving equal status to both family and celibacy.

For a long time evangelicalism has accorded marriage and family a privileged status over celibacy. When a parachurch organization devotes itself to family issues, it risks sending the subliminal message that the preferred Christian way to live is within a nuclear family. Young women who wish to aggressively pursue higher education or careers are warned by their evangelical elders that they are in danger of becoming old maids. Men are suspect if they show little interest in getting married—the assumption being that they must be gay.

On the other hand, Christianity harbors a secret belief that being celibate is actually more spiritual than being married, having children, and enjoying the pleasures of marital sex. The postmodern church will celebrate both the family and celibacy with equal status and enthusiasm.

A biblical case can be made for the spiritual benefits of both individual relationship with God and communal faith. For example, Genesis recounts a series of stories about individuals. Their stories eventually evolved into the Exodus story, in which a community of believers was formed. The Gospels and Acts reveal a similar pattern: Jesus called individuals to become disciples in the Gospels, then in Acts those disciples were organized into a church.

Pluralism and Unity

Theoretically the church is a pluralistic society because it is made up of many members without distinction by class, race, or gender. In reality, however, local churches have been hotbeds of racial tension as well as gender and class oppression. The truth is, we have wanted the whole world to be "like us"—and we have demanded that they become like us if they want us to take their Christian faith seriously.

The postmodern church does not need to be either a melting pot or a smelting pot (one that turns out fabricated believers who all look, think, and act alike). The early church was both Jew and Gentile, slave and master, male and female, with each group retaining its own distinctive characteristics. Spiritually all such divisions dissolve into nothingness, "for you are all one in Christ Jesus" (Galatians 3:28), which means we share equal respect, equal dignity, and equal importance. We all are free to retain our cultural identities, but we must learn how to love and serve those who are different (Romans 14).

The postmodern church is going to have to derive its unity from something other than doctrinal sameness. Of course, there is a baseline of Christian doctrine that people have to profess in order to be called Christian, and Ted Peters, for example, recommends the Apostles' and Nicene Creeds since they represent the bedrock of Christian belief. No doubt we have a long way to go before we see a truly united Christianity, but until we do we should "make every effort to keep the unity of the Spirit through the bond of peace" (Ephesians 4:3).

Protocol and Spontaneity

As churches age, they tend to carry a massive amount of bureaucracy that is sometimes codified in policy manuals. Their procedures and policies, amassed over the years, originally were intended to improve the flow of communication, delineate responsibilities, and expedite decision-making and action. However, later generations find these programs to be archaic and extremely burdensome. Since chaos is characteristic of postmodernity, effective churches will need to respond quickly (even instantly) to opportunities and needs as they arise. Churches that require committee meetings for every dollar spent and every decision made will not keep pace with the rapid changes of postmodern culture. On the other hand, the church never has been and never will be friendly toward anarchy. Therefore, simplistic suggestions that the church "level hierarchies" in favor of networks still need to be reworked so that both the chain of command and informal channels of communication can be maintained.

Church services can be both planned and spontaneous. They are planned in the sense that pastors and worship leaders determine the flow of the service given the background (and liturgy) of their particular church. But no matter how much they plan the music, prayers, Scripture reading, message, rituals, and so on, they *must not try to control the worshiper's experience.* Postmodern churches will leave lots of room for mystery and will make sure their worship has breathing spaces in which the Spirit of God is asked to move.

Irrelevance and Relevance

The megachurch movement has awakened the church to its need for relevance if it is to speak coherently within the world to which it is called. But the emphasis on relevance is one-sided and therefore partly wrong as well as partly right. That's why I am borrowing the polarity of irrelevance and relevance from Paul Hoon's work *The Integrity of Worship.*

When we speak of the church's relevance, we are referring to the church in relationship to secular society. Relevance is not an issue for growing Christians who are willing to learn the church's language and adopt its traditions. Relevance is necessary whenever the church engages the world, whether by witness within the culture or when nonbelievers step inside the church building.

But the church is not oriented exclusively to the world. In the words of Paul Hoon, we accept irrelevance as a "disengagement from the world because it is engagement with a God who is infinitely more than the world."[5]

We are spiritually oriented to God, and this means that our worship is timeless, that it is a participation with other worshipers of the past, present, and future, culminating in the glorious worship in heaven around the throne of God. We do not worry if aspects of our worship are not relevant to our contemporary culture because the larger question of worship is making our lives relevant to God.

Most of the people who attend the church I pastor in California did not grow up singing traditional hymns. The melodies sound strange to ears that have known only contemporary music, and the archaic language puts the meaning of some of the lines beyond the average worshiper. Hymns are certainly irrelevant to popular culture, and the worship leader at our church has struggled to incorporate traditional hymns into our worship.

Nevertheless, hymns—even without being contemporized—add a crucial element to worship: They remind us that we have not invented Christianity but stand within a vast community and tradition that transcends time and space. The historic hymns tie the universal church together around the central themes of our faith.

In Jerusalem there is a church inside the Old City called the Church of Saint Anne. Because of its stone construction and architecture, this church provides wonderful acoustics for a cappella singing. When I travel with a group to Israel, we are seldom in Saint Anne's alone for very long. Usually tour groups from around the world drift in. If we sing worship choruses from our church, then very few people from other churches can join with us. But the times we have sung hymns in Saint Anne's, we have been joined by Christians from every denomination and a variety of nations, and each group is singing the same hymn, yet in its own language. Songs that are outdated by cultural standards still have great power and purpose within the church.

Hymns do not have to be our favorite style of music, and we do not need to completely understand them to feel their power. In some ways their inaccessibility is their strength. We do not know all there is to know about God. When we enter worship, we are surrounded by mystery. Hymns take us out of our own day and age, out of our particular challenges and problems, out of our contemporary culture and place us within the community of believers of all time, worshiping together in the presence of God.

Rational Theology and Experiential Theology

The theology of the modern era has been heavily influenced by the rationalism of the Enlightenment. All in all, this is as it should be, for the Enlightenment set the tone for modern culture, and Christians must meet their culture where it stands. But in many respects Christian theology has been overly rational, to the detriment of the spirit. Clark Pinnock has observed, "Evangelical religion in our day has tended to become overly intellectualized and 'Apollonian.' We have become insecure in the presence of the strange, paralogical powers of the free, dynamic Spirit."[6]

Evangelicals have learned to "test their experience" by the Word of God (which means our rational interpretations of Scripture). What postmodern Christians will also learn to do is to put their interpretations of Scripture to the test of experience. How good is your theology if it does not work in real life? For example, Job's friends espoused a theology that was rationally sound but failed to account for Job's suffering. Try as they might, they could not force Job to squeeze his experience into their simplistic theological formula. Job's experience revealed the flaw of his friends' theology.

Postmodern Christians will need a theology that is rationally sound and true, but they also will need theology to lift them into a state of grace, not forensically but in heart, mind, and spirit. Postmodern theology must direct our lives in the world and also fill our minds with holy reverence that results in worship. Theology will have to be a road map—sometimes rational, sometimes experiential—and not just a dictionary.

Reality and Unreality

A strictly postmodern world would be impossible to live in day to day. In fact, many observers have described the general psychological characteristic of postmodernity as schizophrenic. Postmodernity is a house built upon the sand of *simulacra*—an image with no reality, a sign with no substance. Therefore, it cannot stand.

Nevertheless, the "unreality" of postmodernity creates new possibilities for believers. If postmodernity sees reality as nothing more than a social construction (which to a certain degree is true), then like any other post-modernists, Christians are free to imagine worlds other than the one society imposes on us.

How is the world defined for us now? The difference between our time and the past, according to sociologist Zygmunt Bauman, is that "society once engaged its members primarily as producers. [But] the role that our present-day society holds up to its members is the role of the consumer, and the members of our society are likewise judged by their ability and willing-ness to play along."[7] Our identity in the world is defined by our consumer society.

But the "unreality" aspect of postmodernity—the idea that realities are created by people—permits us to imagine a new identity for ourselves. The ability to dream new worlds is sometimes the only weapon available to a race or class of people who are deprived of power by society. Our willingness to imagine a different world—and ourselves as different persons in that world—enables us to approach the Bible as a new kind of resource (along with all of its conventional uses to our spiritual development). We are able to introduce into our thinking a world built according to Scripture, where our identity is that of God's children.

Once we see ourselves and our world differently, we can begin work-ing for effective changes to bring about a better world. We can use our imaginations to change the script of our lives. This is the path that theologian Walter Brueggeman would set us on:

> The folk in the Bible are shown to be those who have often
> settled into a narrative that is deathly and destructive. Thus the
> early Hebrews had settled for a slave narrative as their proper
> self-preservation. That narrative is disrupted by another narra-
> tive that has Yahweh the liberator as the key and decisive agent.
> The decision to stay in Egypt or leave for the promise is a deci-
> sion about which narrative to follow, whether to understand the
> "plot of life" according to the character Pharaoh or according to
> a different plot featuring Yahweh.[8]

In the permeable reality of postmodernity, we are confronted with the same decision. Do we live as consumer-slaves of society, or do we redefine our lives according to fresh interpretations of Scripture?

The Genesis story of Sodom and Gomorrah has been used as a classic example of God's anger and judgment against moral perversity and especially homosexuality. Christians who never have been tempted by homosexual sin have stood apart from the story, concurred with God's condemnation of those cities, and have stayed untouched personally by that passage of Scripture. But a fresh interpretation of Genesis 18-19 through the eyes of the prophet Ezekiel helps us to see that the detestable behavior of the people of Sodom was symptomatic of their cultural condition, which was marked by arrogance, conspicuous consumption, and a disregard for the poor and needy (Ezekiel 16:49-50).

In a similar manner the story of David and Bathsheba is not only a moral lesson against adultery but a strong rebuke against the misuse of power. The story of the woman caught committing adultery can be interpreted two ways. Looked at in the light of the male accusers, she was treated as an object, a means to entrap Jesus. But Jesus treated her not as an adulteress or sinner but as a person. As long as the woman was being exploited, she had no voice. But once Jesus treated her as a person, she could speak and therefore enter a dialogue with Christ.[9] In postmodern fashion, we will discover that the Bible is capable of yielding many interpretations and that it never stops speaking to contemporary issues.

Tradition and Innovation

Modernity stigmatized tradition as a prison of the soul that humans had to flee if they were to make any progress. The proliferation of Protestant denominations and splinter groups during modernity reveals evangelicalism's lack of esteem for tradition. But what has hurt churches most severely in this area is not that they are without tradition—every institution develops its own—but that they have substituted local, diminutive traditions for the larger and grander traditions of church history.

The postmodern church will have to be both traditional and innovative. There is a way to carry the past with us as we move into the future, like Israel carrying Joseph's mummified bones from Egypt to the Promised Land (Exodus 13:19). If we do not make use of new technologies, our voice in society will be greatly diminished. On the other hand, if we forget our past, if our genealogies do not extend back beyond our own birth, we will forget who we are and where we were going.

Metanarrative and Competing Narratives

In the spiritual marketplace of postmodernity, Christians will have to accept the fact that their story will not be given any special status over other religious stories. For some Christian scholars this is unacceptable, but we are not the ones who determine society's mind-set; we just have to deal with it. On the other hand, Paul gives us an example of how we can position our story so that at least some people who hear it can embrace it as their own.

Paul stood in the heart of the world's spiritual marketplace when he was invited to speak at the Areopagus in Athens. Without slamming his listeners' religions, he introduced Christianity as the overlooked religion and yet the religion with a difference. He used, in fact, one of their own altars for his starting point, and quoted their own poets. Not everyone was convinced, but that is not even a realistic goal. What matters is that everyone there was able to hear in their own context and worldview the message of Jesus Christ in a way they could understand.

Christians must remain loyal to the gospel as the one, true metanarrative—the Story with a capital *S*—handed down to us from God through the Scripture. But we must also respect the narratives of other cultures and religions so that we can maintain a dialogue with them. We must realize that in the eyes of other religions and cultures of the world, our Story appears as just one more story. But even to get our Story heard is a good start. Otherwise we cannot engage the world in dialogue. And as soon as our dialogue ceases, we are building barriers rather than bridges, and our effectiveness in postmodernity dries up.

Other Pairs of Binary Opposites

The church needs to continue to discuss the polarities between modernity and postmodernity so we can choose appropriately which ones to adopt and when to adopt them. Here is theologian and postmodern observer Leonard Sweet's list of "coinciding opposites." I see them as the alternating currents that must run through the church if it is to be energized for postmodern culture. According to Sweet,

> People are moving on the continuum, and I speak here of a
> macramé of complementary, not conflicting or contradictory
> energies, from systematic to narrative, from conceptual to per-
> ceptual, from mechanistic to organic, from monolithic to
> biolithic, from being to becoming, from existential to trans-

personal, from math to image, from nothing-but to as-if, from product to process, from linear to field, from establishment to movement, from hierarchy to network, from private to public, from reductionism to holism, from structure-oriented thinking to process-oriented thinking, from denominational to ecclesial, from means to ends, from theory to fiction, from national to multinational, from eclectic to ecologic, from common sense to intuition, from emotion to volition, from action to character, from divine power to divine presence, from what we know to how we know, from "how much we have" (quantity) to "what we have" (quality), from win/lose to win/win, from authoritar-ian/bureaucratic to cooperative/charismatic, from literalism to multidimensionalism, from system to story, from religious to spiritual, from epic to lyric, from "Here I stand" to "This way we walk."[10]

Revitalizing Worship Symbols

A few years ago a woman began attending church with her twin daughters. Her husband—we'll call him Al—was a big, husky guy who had no use for God. Nevertheless, his wife's faith did not bother him, and he was not concerned that his daughters were "getting religion."

One evening his daughters sat next to him on the couch, waiting for a commercial. When he asked them, "What's up with you guys?" they said, "Daddy, will you please go to our baptism?" It seemed important to them, so he said, "Okay, I'll be there."

At the church service, something happened to Al as he watched people stepping into the water. He saw men like himself descend beneath the surface and reemerge smiling and hugging their friends and family. Al felt an odd emptiness in his chest when his daughters were baptized. Suddenly he was in the water. He did not exactly know what he was doing there, but he knew it was where he wanted to be. He went down and came back up. The change in his life afterward occurred gradually, but it was apparent that he was a different person on a different path.

This story is not unique, nor is it peculiar to postmodernity. But it is indicative of the type of story that will occur more frequently in postmodernity. Al's conversion did not result from an evangelistic program, a rational case for Christianity, or the outreach ministry of a local church. What turned his heart around was the symbolism of one of Christianity's central rituals.

One of the challenges of postmodern faith will be to recover the *sacredness* of our rituals—and this is especially true for Protestants. By and large, modern faith overrationalized the symbols of worship. For example, believers of various traditions have been reminded frequently that the bread and wine of communion are only symbols and not to be taken literally. Reformation reaction to Roman Catholicism has played a major role in de-emphasizing the importance and power of the symbol. So we have been instructed that the power of the sacraments is emblematic and the ritual is powerless and ineffective as a means of grace.

The problem is that the realities of our spiritual existence are invisible and intangible. Symbols provide a bridge between the tangible world of our senses and the intangible world of the Spirit—as the parables of Jesus were a bridge between the common themes of first-century life and the kingdom of God. Modern worshipers have too easily disengaged the symbol from its heavenly referent. If the ritual is made to stand by itself void of God's presence in the elements and movements, then the symbol is drained of its power to evoke higher thoughts, faith, or even the slightest spiritual movement in the heart of the worshiper.

Symbols straddle the earthly reality of which they are made and the heavenly reality that they represent. When approached in reverent faith—

and with an appreciation of their limitations, for the ritual is not magic—they can bring the worshiper into "communion with the Holy and so develop his capacity for adoring love," in the words of Evelyn Underhill. She goes on to say, "But the difficulty of our situation is this: none of these devices will be effective unless the worshiper takes them seriously, far more seriously indeed than in their naked factualness they deserve."[11]

The shallowness of Protestant rituals in modernity was the result of not taking them as seriously as possible. The need for a richer, deeper, more spiritual ritual in postmodernity will push Christians to regard each symbol with the utmost seriousness. To do this, we may need to move our rituals out from under the intense light of reason—which tries to analyze their contents—and treat them as artistic and poetic expressions that are meant to awaken the spirit and, in Underhill's words, "evoke the mysterious." Sometimes we need to allow our rational mind to be transcended by the presence of the holy.

The postmodern church will very likely see a revival of rituals, ceremonies, and sacraments. In their zeal to cut out anything superfluous from Christian faith, the Reformers streamlined the seven holy sacraments of Roman Catholicism and reduced them to just two: baptism and the Lord's Supper. They believed these were the only two rituals to really have the authority of the Lord Jesus. What they deleted were confirmation, penance, extreme unction, holy orders, and the rite of marriage.

Postmodern Christians already are revisiting the discarded sacraments, and we have much to gain by looking again for the sacred, worshipful aspects of marriage, repentance, and confirmation as a rite of passage. The nonrational element of rituals and ceremonies appeal to the postmodern soul. In rituals, *doing* is attached to *believing*—the Word of God is made tangible, and the inner work of God's Spirit is made visible. None of these things requires rational analysis and exposition for postmoderns who are able to enjoy the spiritual value of a ritual as an experience of grace.

Using baptism and communion as examples, I will try to illustrate how we can go about reassessing every Christian ritual, ceremony, and sacrament in order to discover their postmodern currency.

Baptism in Postmodernity

In the summer of 1993, Bill Albrandt took his grandson and granddaughter to North Sterling Reservoir in Colorado to relax in the water and enjoy the sunshine. His grandson, who was three years old, could not swim and drifted into water that was over his head. Being a good swimmer, his eleven-year-old cousin Janean went out to help him. But she had underestimated the strength of his grip as she reached the panicked child. So she screamed to her grandfather, "I can't get him."

Bill dove into the water and swam to his grandchildren. When he reached them, they both immediately grabbed hold of him. He fought desperately to keep their heads above water, but he was unable to move them back to shore. Eventually his strength wore out, and the three of them slipped underneath the water together and drowned.

My father always warned me never to swim up next to a person who had panicked in the water but only to swim close enough to offer him something to grab. When people panic, all they can do is clutch anything that comes near them, hoping to stay afloat. Lifeguards along the California coast never swim up to people in trouble but from a safe distance offer them a plastic buoy attached to a line.

People will be drowning in postmodern culture. The confusion of disparate worlds colliding, conflicting values free-floating through society, and the blurring of the boundary between reality and unreality will overwhelm people. But when they look to religion for answers, the array of alternatives in the spiritual marketplace will simply add to their bewilderment.

Jesus has given His church something to throw to people drowning in the madness of postmodernity. The preserver we throw is the gospel, the good news of God's metanarrative in Jesus Christ. This is something post-modernists can hang on to that will draw them to the safety that is found only in God.

As people sink beneath the surface of postmodernity, the role of the church is to bring them back up, to pull them out of the water. This is the symbolic meaning behind baptism. People go into the water and are pulled up again. There is a momentary death followed by a resurrection. Both baptism and the good news involve being rescued, followed by the gift of new life. "We were therefore buried with him through baptism into death in order that, just as Christ was raised from the dead through the glory of the Father, we too may live a new life" (Romans 6:4).

At twenty-one years old, I was asked to teach a Bible study for young people at an Episcopal church in Southern California. The rector, who was a kind and godly man, took a keen interest in the hundreds of teenagers who filled his sanctuary every Sunday night. On occasion he enjoyed being involved in officiating over communion (Holy Eucharist) or sharing the riches of his church traditions with us in some other way.

One night it occurred to him that these new converts needed to be baptized. He knew that in my background we practiced full immersion baptism—people enter the water and are completely submerged. In his tradition, water is poured on the person three times, in the name of the Father, the Son, and the Holy Spirit.

The rector was more than happy to participate with me in a full-immersion baptism, so we rented a swimming pool at the YMCA and planned the service. "I have a prayer," he said, "that I would like to say over the water." He explained that he would ask the Holy Spirit to hover over the water, to sanctify it, and to bless everyone who stepped into the water to receive baptism.

The prayer raised my awareness of the spiritual significance of baptism. If the water, which had always been only a symbol for me, was actually blessed by God's Spirit, then certainly stepping into it became a more significant act than a mechanical ritual. It became a spiritual rite of passage.

One characteristic of postmodernists is that they are not afraid to dialogue with people who come from backgrounds and belief systems that are significantly different from their own. People should not be forced to participate in a ritual that causes them theological discomfort, but the old antagonisms that kept churches apart in the past need to be revisited to see if we have not erred in our caricatures of people in other churches. Perhaps a postmodern approach to the combining of traditions, cultures, and symbols can help the church not only move toward a greater unity but toward a richer spiritual experience.

The Lord's Supper in Postmodernity

My childhood friend stared into my eyes with all the seriousness an eleven-year-old could muster. We were sitting underneath a row of eucalyptus trees down by the creek. He pulled out a penknife and pricked his finger, then wiped a drop of blood on a rock. "Now you," he said. I courageously duplicated his actions, then together we buried the rock and camouflaged the area.

"We're blood brothers now," he explained. "We will always be true to each other; nothing can ever break our friendship. This is forever."

The fragmented nature of postmodern society will make the bonding aspect of the Lord's Supper a central feature. When Jesus held the goblet of wine before His disciples, He said, "This cup is the new covenant in my blood, which is poured out for you" (Luke 22:20). In effect, He was saying to them, "We're blood brothers now."

When Christians celebrate the ritual of the Lord's Supper (also referred to as Communion or the Eucharist), they are not only "participating" in Christ, but they are bonding with each other. Paul explained, "Because there is one loaf, we, who are many, are one body, for we all partake of the one loaf" (1 Corinthians 10:17). In keeping with Mideastern thought of biblical times, the church as a spiritual community is united by sharing a common meal. This particular meal is not only a collection of symbols but a sacred event.

The bread and the wine are symbols that speak through all the ages (1 Corinthians 11:26). They tell the story of a God who loved His creatures with such a profound and passionate love that He came among them in the person of His Son to live, to heal, to liberate, to enlighten, and to die. And through His death and resurrection, He turns enemies into friends and strangers into brothers and sisters (Ephesians 2:14-19).

The church around the table is a symbolic family, but if the symbol is taken seriously, then the family commitment will remain among the members long after the meal is over. In fact, like family reunions, the meal is simply an opportunity to celebrate our relationships with each other, an excuse to come together to share our lives. Of course, the Lord's Supper is more than a family meal; it is a sacred pact with God. But it is also a family meal.

One goal of the postmodern church will be to celebrate the Lord's Supper in a way that so excites the senses, awakens the spirit, and elicits the mystery of Christ's sacrifice that the person standing on the periphery of the church will say, "All this talk of food is making me hungry," and, "All this talk of family is making me homesick." The sacred meal hopefully will arouse a hunger and homesickness great enough to put the prodigals back on the road that leads to the Father's house.

Symbols for the Spiritually Starved

Before my church's Maundy Thursday service, we attached four large, white panels to the front walls of our sanctuary. Then, while I was speaking, while we were singing, and while we were receiving the Lord's Supper, an artist began painting on those panels.

The first few brush strokes of each painting were indecipherable, like the first bursts of creation. But as the artist continued to add paint and color, symbols emerged, one after another. Just as the service ended, he swept the last stroke across the fourth panel. He had painted four symbols to represent the Last Supper and Good Friday: The bread and the cup, a hammer and nails, a crown of thorns, and finally the Cross.

The added element of visual stimulation and the process of creation enhanced our experience of God's presence in worship. Thus we were drawn deeper into the mystery of Christ's death, deeper into symbols of His love, and deeper into our communion with Him in the bread and the wine.

There are other creative ways to rethink baptism and communion in order to produce fresh and dynamic interpretations of their role in postmodernity. The symbols they contain are elemental, yet powerful: water, bread, blood, and so on. The church that takes those symbols seriously and celebrates them with a dramatic passion will appeal to the spiritually and morally starved soul of postmodernity.

But the postmodern church also will produce new or improvised rituals and willingly will share those innovations with other communities of faith. For example, our church adopted an Easter tradition from a Lutheran church that makes the events of Good Friday and Easter more experiential. All worshipers have the opportunity to personalize the death and resurrection of Jesus, to affix their own sins to His cross, and to celebrate His resurrection.

On Good Friday the sanctuary is dimly lit, and a large, wooden cross is placed on the floor near the center of the room. During the service people write out their sins, suffering, or any other form of sorrow or evil in the world. Then they approach the cross, which may be draped in crimson or simply lies bare, and they either pin or nail their piece of paper to the cross. By the end of the service, the cross is covered with the notes that people have placed there, giving everyone a strong visual representation of the reason Jesus died—a cross literally buried in sin and suffering. The act of pinning one's sins to the cross is very moving.

Sometime before Easter morning, all of the papers are removed from the cross and burned. As people arrive Sunday morning, they bring flowers to place on the cross (or in chicken wire fashioned into the shape of a cross). Before long a huge, beautiful bouquet appears. The beauty of spring and new life reminds us of the fruit of Jesus' suffering, death, and resurrection. In this way rituals have helped us to enter the drama of Christ's passion and resurrection—producing a personal experience of both events—in a way that preaching alone could never provide.

When people drop out of church, one of the most common reasons is that church is boring. The postmodern church will not be—cannot be—boring. Does the church have a creative imagination? If so, then we can devise methods of doing old things in new ways and new things in an exciting way. Otherwise the church will be neither an organization nor an organism. It will simply be obsolete.

Chapter 7

ONLINE WITH GEN X

Now the tax collectors and "sinners" were all gathering around
to hear him. But the Pharisees and the teachers of the law muttered,
"This man welcomes sinners and eats with them."

LUKE 15:1-2

Colin is away at college, but his mom is able to correspond with both of her sons—one in San Diego, the other in Virginia—in real time over the Internet as if passing notes back and forth in the same room. Colin and his brother chose screen names that disguised their true identities, concealing their age and gender. His mother, however, chose to use her real name, a decision that Colin found "disappointingly unoriginal." In an e-mail that he sent to me he said, "Most adults are so confused by the whole thing that they wouldn't understand putting anything but their real name."

He went on to say, "It is interesting how differently the minds of the kids in my generation work since we've been raised on stuff like this. Over the years we've been staring at glimpses of images on television that last fragments of seconds, and our world in general moves incredibly fast. It frustrates me for the most part.

"My friends can hardly listen to a whole song on an album, and you can forget about listening to every song start to finish. They can't stand sports like baseball because of the slow pace, and classical music is out of the question. The musical phrases and progressions are actually complex in classical music and are not constantly grabbing your attention and holding it in place with catchy repetition and speed.

"Another sad result of our society is that most people I know cannot stand just being alone with their thoughts. Just sitting quietly on a bench somewhere and taking in the surroundings can be one of the most therapeutic, regenerating, and enjoyable experiences, but not when it is spoiled by the incessant urge to be 'doing something.'

"However, despite this attention deficit caused by our strobe-lit society, from it we've also gained an incredible ability to do about ninety things simultaneously without feelings of pressure. Sometimes I have about four or five different conversations going on at once on screen, and hidden behind the boxes I am surfing the Web. I'm also usually listening to music, watching television, or sometimes talking on the phone. We are not panicked by chaos, but thrive on it.

"The latest form of communication between me and a friend of mine is talking through headphones. You can go to a Web site and get a system that calls people free of charge, and if you plug a mike or headphones into the microphone jack behind your computer, you can beat the long distance telephone charges."

Welcome to the world of the first generation of postmoderns. For anyone searching for the pulse of this generation, there is a priceless education in Colin's e-mail. Conversation is simulated, identities are virtual, chaos reigns, and an individual's life stretches in many directions at once.

In the sixties, postmodernism began to break through the fissures of society and spread until it redefined the popular culture of Western civilization. Baby boomers and their parents have lived through this transition, but the generation following the boomers was the first to be born into the new postmodern world—the only world they have known. If they look like barbarians to older generations, it is probably because they live in a country that is foreign to their parents and grandparents.

Gen Xers are convinced that their situation is far different from what their parents had to face. And every parent of a young adult remembers having those same thoughts. But never has it been as true as it is today. The life situation of today's young people is radically different from that of their parents, making the old road maps obsolete within the new social landscape.

If there is one big challenge for the people in this first generation of postmodernists, it is for them to find out who they are and where they are going—identity and destiny. Lyle Schaller discerned a rising trend as early as the 1970s, when it became apparent that a dominant social concern had shifted since the Truman generation. "Anyone born before 1945 grew up in a world that stressed survival and in a world filled with institutions that reinforced this concept," Schaller noted. Since that time, however, the cultural need has shifted, and people today are concerned with "identity goals" rather than "survival goals."[1]

One of the implications of pursuing identity goals rather than survival goals, according to Schaller, is that "people are finding more meaning in their lives from recognition and acceptance as persons than from recognition as the performer of a task." But that was back in the seventies, and Schaller was referring to the baby-boom generation. Though the issue of one's identity still is a significant concern, it is a much stickier problem for today's young person.

Who Are They?

They have been called Generation X, though they resist any labels or artificial classifications. They are not one, cohesive group that can be named, but they are many small tribes. In fact, they are millions of independent human beings, each one an isolated niche market. Perhaps this is why the term Generation X (or Gen X) has firmly fixed itself in our current vocabulary. The X represents an unknown quantity in an equation, the factor waiting to be defined when the problem is solved.[2]

Of course, X also can stand for Christ, as in Xmas. But I think this was pretty far from Douglas Coupland's mind when he popularized the term in his novel *Generation X*. Nevertheless, for those of us who are concerned about the mission of the church in the postmodern world, "X marks the spot."

Literature abounds with demographic observations regarding Generation X. Still, I don't believe Gen X can be defined demographically (those born between 1960 and 1980). Members of Gen X are defined more accurately by their postmodern outlook on life than by a definite age range. There is generational spillage on both ends—a few older and a few younger than the Xer age cohort. And there definitely are people within the Gen X age group who do not fit the postmodern profile of their peers (fifty-year-old yuppies trapped in thirty-year-old bodies, perhaps?).

Bill Strauss and Neil Howe did some of the groundbreaking work on Generation X in their books *Generations* and *13th Gen*. To help sharpen our focus, I will briefly review some of their findings and note a few more recent observations.[3]

- Gen X is "the most aborted generation in American history." Millions of their generation never made it into the world.
- Parental divorce has struck Generation X "harder than any other American generation." "Half the kids of divorce recall having felt unwelcome in their new pieced-together families."
- "No other American generation has grown up in families of such complexity." Long gone are the days of *Ozzie and Harriet*. The Gen X model family was the *Brady Bunch*. "At best, divorce brought kids complicated new relationships with moms, dads,

and unfamiliar adults—and new time-consuming hassles shut-
tling back and forth between parents trying to schedule in a little
'quality time' under awkward circumstances."

- "No other child generation has witnessed such a dramatic
  increase in domestic dissatisfaction (and surge to the workplace)
  on the part of mothers." This caused the number of "latchkey
  kids" to nearly double in this generation.
- Teenagers among Gen X committed suicide "more frequently
  than any generation since the Lost [Generation]."
- "The decade of the 1970s brought a steep decline in the economic fortunes of children," and through the 1980s "the economic distress has moved right up the age ladder with them."

Descriptions of Generation X often include the bleak circumstances
they have inherited as they followed the carefree baby boomers into a con-
voluted world. Whereas boomers had free love, Xers inherited AIDS;
boomers returned to nature, Xers have the challenge of saving nature;
boomers experimented with "recreational" drugs, Xers became addicted to
crack and were gunned down in drug- and gang-related shootings; boomers
raised the issue of death as a topic of discussion, and among Xers suicide
and homicide are the leading causes of death.

Gen X has felt (and has been treated) like the child of a divorced couple
that neither parent wants to care for, a burden no matter which home he
enters. Many Xers feel like they have been abandoned, left on the doorstep
of a society that is unwilling to take them in.

Gen X has been stigmatized in the media and among a number of edu-
cators as well. Strauss and Howe present a list of "devil-child horror films"
that were produced about the time that the first wave of Xers arrived in
delivery rooms. They calculated that "A baby born in 1974, the year *It's
Alive!* was released, would have been 18 during the 1992 L.A. riot." Now,
more grown up, Gen X still is portrayed negatively by the media as a slacker,

hacker, low-IQ generation. In an article for the *Atlantic Monthly*, Strauss and Howe reported, "The pop culture conveyed to little kids and (by 1980) teenagers a recurring message from the adult world: that they weren't wanted, and weren't even liked, by the grown-ups around them."[4]

The characters in movies that represent Gen X often are barely articulate, empty-headed losers whose lives are wasted on shallow ambitions. The *Wayne's World / Bill and Ted's Excellent Adventure / Dumb and Dumber* genre of comedies, not to mention the characters Chris Farley and Adam Sandler have portrayed, reflect poorly on this generation. During MTV's run of *Beavis and Butthead*, critics feared that the two violent and moronic delinquent characters were both inspiration for, and a reflection of, today's youth. It's no wonder, according to Strauss and Howe, that Gen X is "cursed with the lowest collective self-esteem of any youth generation in living memory."

Have you ever noticed how sinister looking the future is in sci-fi movies, like some hostile and forbidding wasteland? Tomorrow's world is sometimes depicted as a barren desert or endless sea, where barbarians struggle against natural and mechanical forces for a meaningless survival. The future world of *Blade Runner, Escape From New York, Mad Max, Terminator,* and *The Matrix* are consistent in portraying the future as violence-filled and inhospitable, where biology and technology are merged but not for any good reason. This same world reappears in many cyberpunk novels.

Older adults cringe at the prospect of this sort of future, but Gen Xers calmly regard it with expressionless acceptance. They do not expect their future to be a rosy journey with a romantic ending. Gen Xers accept the world as it is, with all its pain, misfortunes, and apparent injustice. The world is random and dangerous, but it also can be fun if you know how to play the angles and keep yourself emotionally detached.

Gen X entered the job market just as salaries were dropping and taxes were rising. Two generations previous to theirs, a family could purchase a home on a single income. Most boomers have required two incomes to maintain a home. But for Gen X, owning a home is out of the question. "Twenty years ago a typical thirty-year-old male made six percent more than a typical sixty-year-old male; today he makes 14 percent less."[5]

A couple of years ago, Damien, a Gen X college graduate, sent me an e-mail in which he said, "Young people today are considered SUCCESSFUL by their peers if they can simply pay rent in their own space." Further on he added, "What we see here are young people in three categories: (1) Live at home / go away to school on Mom and Dad, (2) Work full time in a 'service' capacity—usually sales, often restaurants, and (3) 'Renaissance' students that make ends meet through a variety of creative sources which may include parental support."

In their book *13th Gen*, Strauss and Howe used a writing device in which they pretended to be posting the contents of their book on a computer bulletin board that is frequently "hacked" into by a Gen Xer whose screen name is "crasher." In one box, crasher comments, "compared to the job market you guys had, we definitely got the smelly end of the plunger. Back in your day, the great questions in life were 'how can I become more self-actualized?' or 'why is there evil when an omnipotent god is good?' for us, they are 'paper or plastic?' or 'would you like fries with that?'"[6]

Back to my friend Damien. His concluding comment on Xer money matters was, "As our economy mutates quicker than the AIDS virus, Xers have to be resilient and adaptable. A swaying reed will outlast a stoic oak when the hurricane comes."

Generation X and Postmodernity

With the demographic data behind us, let's look at this generation through the lens of postmodernity.

Gen X is skeptical of institutions. We have already seen that postmodernism sometimes engages in "destabilizing hierarchies" on behalf of people who have been oppressed by institutionalized power structures. Big corporations and governments that exercise totalitarian-like control over their "subjects" are the bad guys in cyberpunk novels and the target of young computer hackers in popular culture. Xers are not likely to be loyal to the companies that hire them, switching jobs or careers whenever a better opportunity arises. Even though church is not clearly understood by Gen X, organized religion is certainly ranked among the institutions not to be trusted.

Family is vital for Gen X, but Gen X has redefined family. According to Barbara Hargrove and Stephen Jones, "By observation, if not through personal experience, today's youth know that whatever the family may be to them, it cannot be expected to be the solid, unchanging entity that earlier generations assumed and that some contemporaries desperately try to affirm."[7] So family, like everything else in the postmodern world, is a fabrication that people construct for themselves—only Gen X constructs its families intentionally and ironically.

The "Let me introduce you to my dad's ex-wife's stepson" relationships are not the real family with which Gen X identifies. Instead, Xers recreate family within their own peer group, among those they think will understand them best. There is no doubt that the proliferation of gangs, gang symbols, and gang wannabes has been an attempt to fill the void created by the dissolution of families in Western culture. The gang is a family by virtue of its rituals, commitment, and the sense of belonging it fosters.

Gen X collectively and individually carries a lot of raw emotion underneath a veneer of toughness. Xers wear a hard shell to mask their inner griefs and insecurities. They are aware of a rage that constantly is seething inside, but they are not sure about the target that most deserves their pent-up anger. They are even less aware of the other feelings and agonies that lie in a deeper and more remote part of their soul.

In reviewing *Jumping the Green* by Leslie Schwartz, Cornel Bonca peered into the Gen X rage that gave birth to punk culture. He reflected on the reaction of the punk culture to Kurt Cobain's suicide (and specifically the reaction of his wife, Courtney Love). Bonča determined that "punk's toughness was revealed for what it often is: a pile-driver-like aggression as a defense against that terrifying and embarrassing thing called a broken heart."

He went on to say, "Of course, punk is rage against a machine that forces kids to grow up so quickly, so savvily and so unmentored that their natural response is to throw on the thick armor of aggression and cynicism. What happens, though, is that they start to believe their own pose, and they keep it up until something shatters it, whereupon they're stuck holding their naked hearts in their hands, wondering why this strange beating thing hurts so much.... "8

The world of Gen X is "values-free." Xers really have embraced the post-modern position perhaps first espoused by Friedrich Nietzsche that "there are no moral phenomena" but only "moral interpretations." And according to Graeme Codrington, "Sin is a non-issue to today's young people." Codrington's work *Generation X: Who, What, Why and Where To?* is posted on his Web site. It is an excellent resource regarding Gen X.9 If morality, like culture, is something that humans create, then morality also is relative.

They have an ironic and apparently cavalier attitude toward life. This approach to life's challenges, opportunities, and serious problems is perhaps the Gen X characteristic that older adults find most annoying. What the older generations fail to realize is that since childhood, Xers have carried a great deal of stress. First, they have always had to live with rapid change. Second, their broken families have been a source of stress, not only in the dissolution of family bonds but also in the fact that many divorced parents tend to turn to their children with their problems and even seek their advice. Third, they have to cope with difficult economic challenges. And

fourth, they have inherited a troubled world plagued by terrorism and ecological nightmares.

Gen X is the first generation to be wired into the media. They do not
remember the introduction of "Pong"; their video games have always been
action-filled and presented in high-resolution graphics. When computers
became personal, Gen X was given an alternative to a sedentary life in front
of a television screen waiting to be entertained. They became players and
users who were able to participate in the action.

Though Xers are spiritually open, they transform every religion they enter.
They "take religion into their own hands" in three ways, according to Tom
Beaudoin. First, they "live religiously through the popular culture" (what
Beaudoin refers to as their "irreverent spirituality"). Religious symbols have
been utilized in videos, music, movies, magazines, and fashions. Gen X is
aware that spiritual meanings are meant to be evoked—though the interpretation of those meanings is up for grabs.

Beaudoin argues that pop culture is filled with musical images (music
videos), virtual images (cyberspace), and images of the self (fashion). Each
image is a sign that refers to something else. Following a chain of signs will
eventually result in meanings that are primarily religious. As Beaudoin says,
"The more these signs evoke the ground, horizon, or 'limits' of our human
experiences, the more 'religious' our interpretation of the image may be."[10]
Therefore pop culture contains many symbols or images in which Gen X
potentially will discover spiritual meaning.

Second, Beaudoin says, "they have a widespread regard for paganism—
however vaguely defined." Video and role-playing games have introduced
Xers to the world of wizards, witches, and occult magic; feminism has re-
introduced ancient goddess beliefs; and a host of pagan Web sites, books,
and CDs demonstrate the current interest in paganism.

Third, "Xers take religion into their own hands...through a growing

152

enchantment with mysticism.... Xers take symbols, values, and rituals from various religious traditions and combine them into their personal 'spirituality.' They see this spirituality as being far removed from 'religion,' which they frequently equate with a religious institution."[11] The tight logic of Protestant and Roman Catholic theology is not as appealing to Xers as the promise of "experience" that mysticism offers.

A Completely Different World

I cannot stress enough that Generation X has grown up in a world that is very different from any other generation—including the baby boomers.[12] Xers do not know the same "reality" as previous generations: The only world they know is postmodern.

When we decided to host a Gen X ministry through our church, I met with a group of potential leaders. As we were chatting before the meeting began, I asked, "What are the really big issues for your generation? What's out there? What do you hear all the time."

Several people offered one-word answers. Then a young man said, "Real." When I asked him what he meant, he said, "We can't stand posers, people pretending to be something they're not."

As we discussed what it meant to be "authentic," I realized we were speaking a different language. We were using the same words, but they had different definitions.

"Wait a minute," I said. "Are you saying that people can alter their bodies with piercings, tattoos, and implants and still be 'real'?"

"Yes, of course," the chorus of voices came back. I shook my head in bewilderment.

I grew up in the hippie era. The rebellion of my generation against phoniness was a rejection of the "plastic society," consumer articles made to look like wood, metal, or tile, but that were really plastic. To be "real" meant a return to nature. A person's real self was his or her unadorned self (no makeup, no bra, no barbers). A person's natural appearance without any adorning was considered real.

When I asked the Gen X leaders to explain what they meant by real, they replied, "To be true to yourself, who you are on the inside. If someone tries to be something that they're not, then they aren't real." I asked them if someone who dressed gothic—a Hollywood vampire-type look, black clothing, white faces except for black makeup around the eyes—could be "real." "Yes," I was told, "as long as that is who they are on the inside."

Gen X has different definitions for family, values, customs, and just about everything else in popular culture. They also differ from previous generations in the following ways.

The world of Gen X is nonlinear. Modernity was formed by the principles of mathematics—a mathematics that moved in a linear, sequential way; there was always a logical next step. In contrast, the Gen X world is characterized by postmodern chaos. For Douglas Rushkoff, chaos is native territory for his generation and a central theme of his book *Playing the Future.* "Chaos is not mere disorder—it is the deeper order within apparently random, nonlinear systems. Chaos is the character of discontinuity."[13] This is what enables Gen Xers to feel perfectly comfortable doing "ninety things simultaneously without feelings of pressure," as Colin said in his e-mail.

The world of Gen X is unstable and in a constant state of change. The fixed structure of modernity is not giving way to a new fixed structure called postmodernity, but rather to a postmodern flux. Nothing in the world of Gen X holds still. As Colin said, "Over the years we've been staring at glimpses of images on TV that last fragments of seconds." Technological change continues at a mind-boggling pace, music cannot remain popular for more than a few weeks, values have become disposable like other commodities, friends are constantly moving, and families are constantly morphing.

The world of Gen X has no center. The question of the modern era was whether the center could hold when "Things fall apart" and "Mere anarchy is loosed upon the world," according to Yeats. The question of Gen X is, "What center?" In a media-filled culture where political figures are merely "images" molded by spin doctors and every institution is suspect, how does one find a fulcrum, a stable center from which to build a coherent worldview?

The world of Gen X is one in which everyone is entitled to enjoy the best things in life. One of the ramifications of our consumer mentality is that we are customers wherever we go—not just the mall, but also at school, work, and church. As a customer, one has certain expectations regarding service, delivery, and ease of purchase. (I have a Gen X son who feels he has a right to work for a boss who is not a "jerk.")

Gen Xers are products of this culture, and they feel they are owed something by society—first, because advertisers create the illusion that the good life is within everyone's reach. And second, because if they have to pay for a college education, then they deserve (by virtue of their purchase) a decent grade from each class (to guarantee graduation and a career that will provide them access to hyper-consumption). So when their way is barred at any point, they feel wronged.[14]

The world of Gen X is void of absolute truth. In the hyper-real world of media images and sound bytes, truth loses its universality and objectivity, becoming instead personal and subjective. Gen X does not look for truth in religion, science, or philosophy but in personal experience, intuition, and assumption. Xers are skeptical of people who make claims to the truth and wonder what it is they are trying to sell.

Gen X is prepared for the world that has been prepared for them. Older adults tend to look to the future with apprehension, if not dread. We constantly are reminded of the world's swelling population, the deforestation of the planet, ozone depletion and the corresponding global warming, the fact that small and politically unstable countries have developed nuclear weapons, and that government seems to move slowly and ineffectively. The future we envision is a social and political nightmare.

Douglas Rushkoff suggests that there is another way to look at the future. If we want to see something other than "decline, decay, and death," then it may be that "we have no choice but to adopt the open-mindedness of youth." In his book *Playing the Future,* Rushkoff argues that our children are adapted to deal with the world of the twenty-first century. "Our kids are younger and less experienced than us, but they are also less in danger of becoming obsolete. They are the latest model of human being. Looking at the world of children is not looking backward at our own past—it's looking ahead."[15]

Colin is not bothered by the multitasking he has to perform to simultaneously maintain several online conversations, watch television, and do his homework. Damien is not afraid to substitute teach and work a variety of "McJobs" until a full-time teaching position becomes available. And Will is not afraid to sit down in front of a computer and boot up a program he has never seen run before. Young people do not need to adapt to the times, they *are* the times.

When missionaries enter a new culture, they have to make adjustments to embrace the language, manners, and customs of that culture. Children born to missionaries, or who are taken into new cultures while very young, do not have to make those adjustments; their surroundings are not "foreign" to them, and they grow up enculturated to that environment (and often learn the language faster and with greater fluency than their parents).

Our children are native to the postmodern world. Though we find it difficult to adjust to the new realities, they find them normal. As Alan Kay observed, technology is "technology only for people who are born before it was invented." The computer is not technology for my children any more than a shovel is for me. For better or worse, the new world is theirs.

Postmodern Prodigals

We do not need to stretch our imaginations to find important spiritual lessons regarding Generation X in the biblical story of the prodigal son. Looking at this story, we must first remind ourselves that Jesus conceived this parable because a group of crabby religious people on the fringe of His ministry felt His concern for "sinners" was inappropriate. The prodigal son story was the third of three—a shepherd's lost sheep, a widow's lost coin, a father's lost son—all of which carried the same message, that the proper response to recovering something that was lost is joyful celebration.

Leaving Home

Here is how Jesus' story about the prodigal son begins:

> There was a man who had two sons. The younger one said to
> his father, "Father, give me my share of the estate." So he divided
> his property between them.
>
> Not long after that, the younger son got together all he had,
> set off for a distant country and there squandered his wealth in
> wild living. After he had spent everything, there was a severe
> famine in that whole country, and he began to be in need. So he
> went and hired himself out to a citizen of that country, who sent
> him to his fields to feed pigs. He longed to fill his stomach with
> the pods that the pigs were eating, but no one gave him any-
> thing. (Luke 15:11-16)

It is widely known that Generation X has little tolerance for organized religion. But the truth is they have little understanding of the church and tend to confuse any sort of Christian community with heavy-handed authoritarian hierarchies. For the most part, Gen X has little real experience of church, knowing it mostly from what they have seen in the movies and on television.

American history has shown a fairly stable pattern of church attendance within every generation. In childhood, youth are dragged to church. When they reach adolescence, they stop attending, but when they become young adults, get married, and have children, they return to church. Thus the majority of each generation of Americans has had some kind of church experience. Until now.

Baby boomers became the first generation that did not return to church in adulthood. True, there were brief spikes in boomer church attendance, but those proved to be temporary, experimental ventures into mainstream denominations. Most of the boomer generation stayed away from church. Therefore Gen X is the first generation of Americans who have entered adulthood with no religious background. You will find that when you mention the word *church* to them, you receive a blank stare. "What's the point?" they ask. "Why would someone want to do church?"

Outside of religious institutions, Gen X searches for something big enough to give meaning to life. Unfortunately, their search flounders in the postmodern void where every path is as good (or as bland) as any other and nothing is considered more significant, more important, or more holy than anything else. Not surprisingly, like the prodigal of the New Testament, the Gen X quest often has led to "wild living."

Gen X has given the world a new appreciation of sport—though its gladiatorial aspects hark back to the past. Xers have taken sport—mostly individual activities rather than team play—to a new level. They have added all kinds of acrobatic stunts to bicycling, skateboarding, skydiving, and skiing, and even added several new dangerous sports, including snowboarding, in-line skating, and bungee jumping. The idea behind this quest for excitement is to come so close to the edge of life (or death) that they experience what a rush it is to be alive. One popular culture expression of this extreme need for excitement is the movie *Flatliners,* where medical students assist each other in brief excursions into death followed by resuscitation.

Listen to the commonly used superlatives of the Gen X vocabulary, which from their youth have included "awesome" and "radical" and now include "extreme" and "outrageous." They want to experience life without boundaries or limits. They even chafe against the boundary imposed by death.

But, like the prodigal son, Gen Xers are suffering from a "severe famine." The famine is identical to the one foreseen by the prophet Amos: "'The days are coming,' declares the Sovereign LORD, 'when I will send a famine through the land—not a famine of food or a thirst for water, but a famine of hearing the words of the LORD. Men will stagger from sea to sea and wander from north to east, searching for the word of the LORD, but they will not find it'" (Amos 8:11-12).

The Word of the Lord is what gives people a spiritual basis for their lives. It creates meaning, hope, and moral relevance. The Word of the Lord is the revelation from God that makes sense out of the chaos, that provides light through the darkness, that feeds the starving souls of people who have come to the end of human culture and have been left empty.

A life without boundaries, without moral commitment, without limits is a hard life to maintain. Individuals must constantly try to determine if they have gone too far or not far enough. They can never rest. Total freedom has negative side effects.

For all their celebrated playfulness and irony, Gen X is spiritually starving in a secular wasteland where they sometimes try to feed their souls on media icons, which contain at best a quasi-spirituality. Like the prodigal, they long to fill themselves on anything that might satisfy their incessant craving, but no one is likely to give them anything that will satisfy them—just as the prodigal, who was starving but "no one gave him anything."

Finding a Way Back

Despite the challenges, there is great hope for this generation because life without boundaries often leads back home. Listen as Jesus unfolds the story of the prodigal:

> When he came to his senses, he said, "How many of my father's hired men have food to spare, and here I am starving to death! I will set out and go back to my father and say to him: Father, I have sinned against heaven and against you. I am no longer worthy to be called your son; make me like one of your hired men." So he got up and went to his father. (Luke 15:17-20)

One of the biggest challenges facing Gen Xers is the task of finding their identity and destiny. This is an individual quest that requires ample social interaction, support, and encouragement. Since our culture does not reward personal and spiritual growth, this becomes an even more difficult task.

In *Continental Philosophy since 1750,* Robert Solomon tracked the role and place of the human self in philosophy from the Romanticists to the present. He concludes that the self has been done away with in postmodernism. If people discover a vacuum inside where once there lived a soul, they are in danger of having some other, external force define who they are. Generation X is especially vulnerable to having the self defined by culture as nothing more than a consumer.

Robert Lifton and more recently Martin Marty have used the term *Protean Man* to describe the way the postmodern self is able to morph into so many diverse identities. Gen Xers have perfected the protean style and can shift into a new identity almost every time they turn around. They are able to hold a variety of conflicting opinions without feeling the discontinuity of their incoherence. Their lives consist of random images and disconnected narratives. For example, when the Fugees did a remake of Roberta Flack's song *Killing Me Softly*, they did not try to match the lyrics to the video. The song itself is a ballad, and the story it tells is specific and moving. The video, however, has nothing to do with the lyrics of the song. The visual image unfolds its own story while the words of the song move through it like oil in vinegar.

That the video images do not match the story of the song is insignificant to both the artists and the audience. But the apparent incongruity typifies the members of this generation—they find their own congruities in nontraditional ways.

Cathy Stratton directs the children's ministry in our church. For one season she took a job collecting tickets at the nearby Irvine Meadows Amphitheater. She felt that doing this would give her a deeper insight into the conflicts, issues, and needs of young people. She also was able to attend rock concerts for free.

One evening Cathy was standing near an exit listening to the band when a young man approached her. Apparently he wanted to impress Cathy, so he began to divulge to her his philosophy of life. "I believe love is the strongest force in the universe," he said. "If everyone would just love everybody else, we could solve every world problem."

Then in the next breath he began bragging of his skill in martial arts. He said to Cathy, "Do you see that guy over there? I could easily go over there and break his leg. Do you wanna see me break his leg?" Cathy later described the remarkable way this young man was able to shift from one point of view to the exact opposite without any sense of the radical incongruity of his statements.

In the *New International Version* of the New Testament, we are told that the young prodigal "came to his senses" (Luke 15:17), which interprets the more literal translation of the *King James Version:* "And when he came to himself." He found himself, his true self, while starving in the distant country.

One of the great challenges of Generation X will be that of identity—the formation of an authentic sense of the self. But the danger is that Xers will attempt to define themselves with only the means available to them within popular culture. For example, introspection is frequently presented as the method for finding one's self, to "go within"—often guised as a spiritual journey. However, Barbara Hargrove and Stephen Jones point out that given the social nature of the self, "introspection is a poor way to discover who you are."[16] Some psychological theorists are saying that we discover our true self in the web of our personal relationships.

The prodigal, however, discovered himself when he began to reflect on his father and his father's house. This is significant for two reasons: First, identity is a composite of history plus memory, and second, identity is a gift of God and is formed in relationship with Him—God being the One represented by the forgiving father in Jesus' parable.

Since identity is a composite of history plus memory, without a memory of your personal history you are nobody. If you lose your memory, you lose your identity. As we read the history of Israel in the Bible, we see that the collective memory created for the Hebrews an identity as a people, and the fact that they maintained their identity through nearly two thousand years of not having a national homeland speaks for its strength. Postmodernists who are able to tie in to the history of Scripture and feed it into their memory will stand an excellent chance of building stable identities.

Second, Scripture tells us that God gives the gift of personal identity and that it is formed in the context of a relationship with Him. He is a God who gives names, and the name He gives—to Abraham, Sarah, Jacob, Solomon—becomes the individual's identity. There is real value in seeking our identity in God rather than through introspection or popular culture. Finding out who we are begins with the discovery of the One who called himself "I AM WHO I AM" (Exodus 3:14).

As we go through life, we pick up emotional baggage, survive crises, and experience painful events. As a result our personalities are twisted by our experiences so that our authentic self is lost to us. Only God knows our true self. Only God can help us become our true self.

The Bible challenges us to live up to our "new self" in Christ (Ephesians 4:24; Colossians 3:10). The new self is who you are when all the lies and pain and failures of the twisted old self have been washed away. For example, in Philippians 3 Paul came up with an impressive list of personal accomplishments, but he came to realize that was not his true self. His identity did not depend on his performance, and he turned his back on his accomplishments in order to find himself in Christ. We live the warped life of the old self only if we do not discover, or have forgotten, our true self.

Generation Xers will begin to discover who they truly are when they get up and head to their Father's house.

A Party at the Father's House

> But while he was still a long way off, his father saw him and was filled with compassion for him; he ran to his son, threw his arms around him and kissed him. The son said to him, "Father, I have sinned against heaven and against you. I am no longer worthy to be called your son."
>
> But the father said to his servants, "Quick! Bring the best robe and put it on him. Put a ring on his finger and sandals on his feet. Bring the fattened calf and kill it. Let's have a feast and celebrate. For this son of mine was dead and is alive again; he was lost and is found." So they began to celebrate. (Luke 15:20-24)

Now we come to the role we can play as the church in helping Gen Xers find a faith in their turbulent postmodern world. The actions of the father in the story are an idealized version of the way believers should welcome newcomers into the family of God. Unfortunately for us, we will find that

163

much of the father's behavior goes against our instincts as upright and responsible church members. For example, the father immediately felt compassion for his son, embraced him, and kissed him. We may find ourselves, however, shrinking away from Xers who have treated their hair and bodies like pieces of art. Or if their retro-greaser look does not put us off, their irreverent attitude and behavior may disturb us. The truth is, we do not want them to come home as they are. We want them first to take a bath and put on some decent clothes.

A pastor of one of America's megachurches hired a young man to begin a Gen X ministry in his church. The young man had built up a significant ministry of mostly Gen X members in another city, and the megachurch pastor felt he was qualified to take on the challenge of helping his predominantly baby-boomer church reach the next generation.

The Gen X minister went to work, and in a short while he had not only developed a significant ministry, but he also had gained notoriety as being somewhat of an expert regarding the spiritual needs of Generation X. Before long he realized he had a significant difference of opinion with the senior pastor regarding where his Gen X ministry was going.

The Gen X minister had envisioned a ministry separate from the megachurch, one that could define its own goals, values, and future according to the Gen X culture. The senior pastor, however, was looking for something else. He wanted a Gen X ministry that eventually would fold Xers into the life of the boomer church, helping them to become clean, healthy, and productive members. In other words, he had hired the Gen X pastor to civilize the barbarians and train them to become tithers.

Because the postmodern culture is not like any other the world has ever seen, we need to realize that Gen X ministry will not be identical to any other kind of ministry we have seen before. We are looking at a new world, and that requires new strategies. I have colleagues who wonder if the church in its present form even has a hope of surviving the twenty-first century.

In Luke 15, the prodigal wandered off to a distant country in search of fun and excitement. But when he returned, he discovered how much fun he could have in his father's house. The father said, "Let's have a feast and celebrate." The older son, who always had faithfully served his father, had never experienced a party like this one to welcome back the straying brother.

Interestingly, the father did not begin laying down rules for the prodigal, nor did he tell him how life was going to change for him now that he was home. Instead he filled his home with music and dancing (verse 25), the kind of activities he believed his son would enjoy.

The Gen X church will look different from the church as we know it now. Xers will likely want to bring their raw emotional energy into worship. This is the generation that invented moshing, and they will need a style of worship that helps them feel and release their emotions, especially their anger and hurt. They will need an environment where they can freely express themselves in laughter and tears. Their churches will be dynamic rather than static, experiential rather than cerebral, and more like a party than a funeral.

Churches must reexamine the way they respond to Generation X and how much allowance they will give this generation to develop its own forms of worship, its own ways of studying the Bible, and its own ways of practicing the faith. Will our churches host the party for Xers who want to return to the Father? The problem, staying to the story of the prodigal, is that most of our churches are not under the administration of the father, but of the older brother.[17]

Gen X needs more latitude than what "older-brother" Christians are willing to give. Unfortunately, older-brother religion is seriously out of step with contemporary culture. Some Christians take pride in this fact, but that is because they do not realize their backwardness is not theological but cultural, and there is a price to pay for dissociating one's self from mainstream culture. The more extreme prohibitions of fundamentalist Christianity no longer make sense. If we force Gen X to maintain a psychological distance from popular culture, we create tensions that are unnecessary, psychologically harmful, and unbiblical. Can we really justify doing this again to yet another generation? What we need is not a Christianity that avoids culture but one that disciples us in ways that enable us to navigate culture.

One of the greatest services the church can provide for Gen Xers is to encourage them to stay close to popular culture as evangelists, not missionaries. The difference is that a missionary is basically a foreigner. Gen X Christians should be encouraged to be conversant (and engaged if they feel so inclined) in all of the following:

- the intellectual climate of popular culture
- the music, film, art, and literature of popular culture
- significant events
- the various "tribes"
- trends, fashions, and movements

Perhaps the most serious issue for Gen X Christians is to discern where God is at work in popular culture and what inroads He is creating for introducing the truth of Jesus Christ.[18] Our typical cultural withdrawal removes us from spaces in society where Christian presence is most needed, depriving popular culture of our particular point of view.

Having grown up in a strict, religious subculture, I sat out of most of the important events of my own generation: its rallies, marches, sit-ins, concerts, and festivals. I barely knew the political issues or celebrities of popular culture. My generation was turning society upside down, but I was watching it happen from the sidelines, as though I were a spectator watching a passing parade.

Everything valued by my religious subculture was unknown in the mainstream culture where I spent most of my life (i.e., school). Even other Christian teenagers had no idea what speaking in tongues meant. It sounded spooky to them. (One Presbyterian friend thought it was a communist plot.) On the other hand, everything that was apparently valued in mainstream culture—parties, alcohol, chasing girls—was taboo in my religious world. I felt an excess of guilt for even hearing people talk about what they wanted to do on the weekend.

I knew I was different from other people in my generation, so I tended to isolate myself. I could not see through the taboo behavior of many of my peers to recognize their good hearts. What shocked me most about my twenty-year class reunion was the number of people in my graduating class who had become devout Christians—they all seemed so pagan in high school. But I had been looking at them through a hyper-religious lens.

Because I was embedded in a religious subculture in high school, I felt discomfort with my daily environment. Of course, being a teenager (and not too swift), I internalized my discomfort and concluded that I was an odd person, a misfit, and indeed I became odd. I wish my story were unique. It is not.

We need to let Gen Xers know it is possible to be in the world, yet not of the world. It is possible to live in popular culture without being committed to its values, obligated to its sins, or defined by its worldview. Conversion does not mean a retroversion to modernity—a past that means little to children born since the sixties. Xers will need churches that can assist them in their work in popular culture, encourage them to engage their generation in ways that allow them to represent Christ without resorting to odd behavior.

The Older Brother's Anger

Jesus' story continues with the reaction of the prodigal's older brother:

> Meanwhile, the older son was in the field. When he came near
> the house, he heard music and dancing. So he called one of the

servants and asked him what was going on. "Your brother has come," he replied, "and your father has killed the fattened calf because he has him back safe and sound."

The older brother became angry and refused to go in. So his father went out and pleaded with him. But he answered his father, "Look! All these years I've been slaving for you and never disobeyed your orders. Yet you never gave me even a young goat so I could celebrate with my friends. But when this son of yours who has squandered your property with prostitutes comes home, you kill the fattened calf for him!"

"My son," the father said, "you are always with me, and everything I have is yours. But we had to celebrate and be glad, because this brother of yours was dead and is alive again; he was lost and is found." (Luke 15:25-32)

Traditionally, the church has been skeptical of the youth. Typically churches have tried to create programs to attract Gen Xers, isolate them from popular culture, and work on civilizing them. In the words of writer and social commentator P. J. O'Rourke, the message of most churches to Gen X is, "Pull your pants up, turn your hat around, and get a job."[19]

Because of the sibling rivalry that has gone on between boomers and Xers, we can expect some resistance to authentic Gen X ministry from boomer-run churches. Xers have some justification for their grudge against boomers. In the eyes of Generation X, every phase of life was terrific when the baby boomers entered it and a wasteland when they left.

Bill Strauss and Neil Howe report that boomers tend to preach at Xers, to scold them for not working hard enough to make something of their lives.[20] Smitten with the older-brother syndrome, boomers are not likely to make many accommodations to Xers.

Boomers were cultural innovators in their adolescence, experimenting with drugs and demonstrating against the government. They opened the door to many new experiences. Xers, following in their tracks, found everything slightly warped, not as lovely and much more harsh. Now boomers yell at Xers, "You've gone too far!" and Xers shout back, "You left the door open! You swept through society like locusts, and we're lucky to eat the crumbs you left behind."

Boomers and Xers may seem too close in age to be separated by a generation gap, but as Lyle Schaller explained, "What has so often been described as a generation gap is not a gap between generations as much as it is a difference between perspectives and value systems."[21] Two generations are stepping into the future together, and one is shouting, "Just say no!" while the other is screaming, "Just do it!"

In Jesus' parable, the father's goal was to reconcile the brothers but especially to convince his older son that he should rejoice in his brother's return. The brothers were different, but they both were loved by their father and had a relationship with him. The purpose of the parable was to teach those of us who are "older brothers" how to respond to the salvation of our younger, sinful, and strange-looking siblings.

If churches can assist Generation X in these endeavors and stand nearby ready to support them, then popular culture will not "go to the devil" but will have within it a redeeming presence that will operate through the power of God in a biblical, albeit postmodern, way. In postmodern fashion, Gen X churches are likely to borrow from a lot of different Christian sources. Expect them to plunder many traditions, to mix liturgy with spontaneous prayers, hymns (drums included) with contemporary choruses, and Celtic devotion with Benedictine spirituality. If you are an older-brother believer, expect Gen Xers to worship God in ways that make you feel uncomfortable. But, so long as they are faithful to historic Christian teaching, don't interfere with them or criticize their relationship with God. Rather, rejoice that they have returned to the Father.

Gen Xers are equipped to do God's work in the postmodern world. They are not afraid to enter it either in person or by modem. God has prepared a new generation for this era, and I am certain He will be pleased if His older sons and daughters stand ready to be joyful mentors and sponsors.

Chapter 8

STORYTELLERS AND SOUL HEALERS

Jesus spoke all these things to the crowd in parables;
he did not say anything to them without using a parable.

MATTHEW 13:34

It was midafternoon, and we were looking for shade in the busy promenade on Ben Yehuda Street. I had spent the morning with Craig and Bill wandering inside the walls of Jerusalem, preparing for a special tour we would host the following month. Having finished our business early, we decided to enjoy some Middle Eastern culture before returning to our hotel. That's how we found ourselves on Ben Yehuda Street, a lovely stretch of shops cordoned off to car traffic, where street musicians play for coins and vendors display jewelry, paintings, and handcrafted items.

If you are hungry, Ben Yehuda Street is the place to go. There you will find falafels and schwarmas, if you care to experience the local flavor, or you can eat at Pizza Hut or McDonald's if you crave the taste of home. We chose ice cream. We sat down underneath a colorful umbrella and rested our weary legs. That is when the shouting started.

Standing in the middle of a large open square, a tall bearded man with a floppy hat began preaching loudly. He was wearing a burlap vest, perhaps to mimic the sackcloth of penitence that appears so frequently in the Old Testament. However, this modern-day prophet wore a T-shirt under the burlap.

He was proclaiming the end of the world. God was angry with the nations and was about to send His fire on the planet. People would occasionally turn their heads in the direction of this strange man, as if to see what all the commotion was about. But no one stopped to listen. After all, he was preaching in English!

The street preacher was broadcasting his message, but was he communicating? Was anyone *receiving* his message? He could have been more effective if he had spoken Hebrew, and even more effective if he had taken the time to build relationships with the people, learn their culture, address their needs, speak in a rational manner, and wear normal clothing. Instead, he appeared to be just another misguided oddball.

The world is changing, a new society is emerging, and we are being carried into it. As in every generation since the time of Christ, we have a message from God for our world. I am certain that the Christian church will be faithful to deliver the message, but will anyone receive it? Will we be able to communicate effectively in postmodernity?

It is time to outline a strategy for Christian communication in a postmodern context. How can we speak so that people will listen? And how can we present the truth of Scripture so the Christian message recovers the credibility it lost in modern times?

Perhaps the operative word for facing the challenge of postmodern Christian communication is *innovation*. Jesus said the teacher who has "been instructed about the kingdom of heaven is like the owner of a house who brings out of his storeroom new treasures as well as old" (Matthew 13:52). Postmodernity presents us with challenges and questions that modernity is not equipped to answer. So even though we need to remain well-connected to tradition and history (the "old treasures"), we also must be concerned with originality (the "new treasures").

On a positive note, postmodern communication is usually a lot of fun. Other than the technical writing of intellectuals and academics, postmodern literature is imaginative, playful, humorous, and ironic. Nevertheless, postmodern communication requires a lot of thought, work, and—for our purposes—integrity. A postmodern audience will not buy the same tired, old answers of modern-era Christianity in repackaged form.

Paul's Cultural Wisdom

Look closely at the following two passages and see if you can discern Paul's method for connecting with his audience in two different cities. In the first instance Paul was preaching in a Jewish synagogue in Antioch, and in the second he was at the city gates of Lystra.

> Men of Israel and you Gentiles who worship God, listen to me!
> The God of the people of Israel chose our fathers; he made the
> people prosper during their stay in Egypt, with mighty power he
> led them out of that country, he endured their conduct for
> about forty years in the desert, he overthrew seven nations in
> Canaan and gave their land to his people as their inheritance. All
> this took about 450 years. (Acts 13:16-20)

> Men, why are you doing this? We too are only men, human like
> you. We are bringing you good news, telling you to turn from
> these worthless things to the living God, who made heaven and
> earth and sea and everything in them. In the past, he let all
> nations go their own way. Yet he has not left himself without

testimony: He has shown kindness by giving you rain from
heaven and crops in their seasons; he provides you with plenty
of food and fills your hearts with joy. (Acts 14:15-17)

Paul delivered two different messages to two different audiences; one
Jewish and the other Gentile. He made particular statements and references
to his Jewish audience that he deleted from his message to the Gentile audience. Let's look at these differences side by side:

THE SYNAGOGUE OF ANTIOCH (Acts 13:13-41)	THE GATES OF LYSTRA (Acts 14:15-17)
How Paul addressed them: *"Men of Israel"* *"Brothers, children of Abraham, and you God-fearing Gentiles" (13:26)*	How Paul addressed them: *"Men"*
How Paul referred to God: *"The God of the people of Israel"*	How Paul referred to God: *"The living God who made heaven and earth"*
What Paul said about history: *God worked through Israel's history to produce the Messiah.*	What Paul said about history: *God let all the nations go their own way.*
How Paul related to them: *"My brothers" (13:38)*	How Paul related to them: *"We too are only men, human like you."*

This is Paul's method of evangelism in action, a method he described in
1 Corinthians 9:19-23:

Though I am free and belong to no man, I make myself a slave
to everyone, to win as many as possible. To the Jews I became
like a Jew, to win the Jews. To those under the law I became like
one under the law…so as to win those under the law. To those
not having the law I became like one not having the law…so as
to win those not having the law. To the weak I became weak, to
win the weak. I have become all things to all men so that by all
possible means I might save some. I do all this for the sake of the
gospel, that I may share in its blessings.

Paul tailored his message—and his lifestyle—to his audience. He spoke
to Jews in the context of their religion, culture, and history. He spoke to
Gentiles in a much broader context. The content of his message was always
the same, but it was packaged differently for each audience.

Paul was careful to speak in terms that were most relevant to the culture
and context of his audience. In every case, Paul's primary concern was winning and saving people through the message of Jesus' death and resurrection. If Paul made compromises to relate to people, his compromises were
only cultural. He never compromised his integrity, theology, or the message
of the gospel.

There is one other important difference between the two messages Paul
delivered in Acts 13 and 14. Paul quoted from the Old Testament Scripture
to his Jewish audience (13:33-35), but he did not quote Scripture to the
Gentiles. Instead, the "testimony" of God to the Gentiles is seen in His
"kindness" (14:17). When in Athens, Paul quoted from poets familiar to his
listeners (Acts 17:28). He did not quote Scripture to Gentile listeners for
the simple reason that they did not recognize its authority. The Bible is a
source of evidence and proof only for people who already accept its authority.

This is not to say that God never uses Bible verses to speak to non-Christians. The Holy Spirit has many tools at His disposal for awakening the heart and soul of a nonbeliever. The power of God's truth can "cut to the quick" when expressed in a persuasive argument, a compelling story, or a quoted Bible verse so long as the Spirit of God is guiding the person who is speaking (see Ephesians 6:17). There certainly is power in the Word of God, especially for the spiritual formation of His people (e.g., 2 Timothy 3:14-17; Hebrews 4:12). But many non-Christians who do not accept the authority of the Bible will dismiss our arguments if all we do is quote verses. It is the truth of Scripture we want them to discover, and sometimes we must guide them to the point where they are ready to accept its truth so that it will go to work within them.

Paul's method of evangelism teaches us our first lesson in becoming effective in postmodernity. We have to learn to speak in the language, thought, experience, and culture of the people with whom we wish to communicate. We have to translate the message of the Bible into terms they understand. If people hear and understand the gospel and then reject it, they are responsible for their decision. But if they never understand the gospel because no one ever made it clear to them, then their rejection is due in part to the failure of the communicators.

We do not realize how much we have been exactly like the "prophet" I heard ranting on Ben Yehuda Street. We assume that because we speak English, everyone in our culture will understand us. But our Christian vocabulary, the Bible, and our rituals and church life all are foreign to most people outside the church.

There is a chapter in John Stott's book *Between Two Worlds* entitled "Preaching as Bridge-Building." In this chapter Stott describes the wide gulf between the ancient world and today. He writes: "It is across this broad and deep divide of two thousand years of changing culture (more still in the case of the Old Testament) that Christian communicators have to throw bridges. Our task is to enable God's revealed truth to flow out of the Scriptures into the lives of the men and women of today." Unfortunately, a lot of our preaching "fails to build a bridge into the modern world. It is biblical, but not contemporary."[1]

The challenge of communication is always the challenge of building a bridge across what Chuck Kraft calls a "communication gap." Kraft argues that to bridge the communication gap, the communicator must be "well connected" on both sides of the gap. For us this means being fluent enough in Scripture that we can easily translate it to others, and being sufficiently in touch with popular culture to address its needs.[2] What good is a faith that is active and functional only in church and Bible classes? Is God really concerned with how much information we can acquire? What do you suppose is God's preference; that we examine the Christian life from several different perspectives or that we live it? Do our debates over Hebrew and Greek words glorify Him or help promote His will in the world? If we can learn instead to speak to the challenges of Christian living in a postmodern world, we will be able to communicate with nonbelievers while at the same time providing older believers spiritual answers to our daily struggles and temptations.

If we are going to have any influence for God in popular culture, we cannot be lazy. We cannot sit in front of our television screens whining about how violent and evil the world has become. There are several disciplines we need to master until we can perform them naturally. Those disciplines are an authentic engagement with Scripture, with other believers, with popular culture, and with nonbelievers.

Authentic Engagement with Scripture

There is no Christianity apart from the sacred text of the Bible. Therefore our first task is to work at a more authentic and intense engagement with Scripture. Believers who think we need to move away from the Bible to appeal to postmodern culture underestimate the power of God's revelation and its startling relevance to contemporary issues. We need more of the Bible, not less.

The Christian church has every right to a "sacred text" in postmodernity. The postmodern arguments intended to legitimate various ethnic groups, minorities, and subcultures also stress the right of each tribe to adhere to its own sacred text. Regardless of what anyone else thinks of the Bible, postmodern Christians are accorded the right to read it and apply it however they desire. There is no battle in this regard.

What we need now are fresh interpretations of Scripture. Christians tend to read the Bible again and again but always see the same things. This is because we have been reading each other's commentaries and Bible study guides. The modern engagement with Scripture was mostly intellectual: the quest for information—an obsession with facts, dates, ancient manuscripts, and systems of doctrine. Ministers became renowned if they were good Bible teachers, and many pursued the goal of being the person with all the right answers. Serious Christians became "students" who learned the various methods of Bible study or lined their shelves with biblical dictionaries and reference works.

We need to deepen our understanding of the Bible, but we need more. We need to get outside our religious subcultures and hear how the Bible speaks to other cultures. By hearing the Bible read in voices that are unfamiliar to us, the voices of people who have been abused, neglected, or marginalized, we begin to see new meanings and powerful applications.

Chuck Kraft had his eyes opened to fresh biblical interpretations when he went to Africa. Chuck and his wife, Meg, moved to Nigeria anxious to bring God's truth to the village church that he pastored. He felt the most important New Testament book to teach was Romans, insomuch as it revealed the essential message of salvation by grace through faith. But try as he might, he could not get his congregation interested in studying Romans with him or elicit more than a yawn when he began teaching.

On the other hand, when he read stories from the Old Testament, his listeners were on the edge of their seats. They even begged him not to skip over the genealogies, which to them were the most important part of the story. After all, their culture for many years had been haunted by the spirits of their ancestors. Genealogies gave the Bible a credibility for them that no argument could have established.

Kraft discovered that when he read Old Testament stories, his audiences usually found lessons that were different from those he had been taught in his Western biblical education. When he told the story of Jacob's son Joseph, who was taken to Egypt as a slave, Kraft wanted to stress the importance of Joseph's strength to resist the temptations of Potiphar's wife. His church members, however, saw Joseph as a hero and a righteous man because "he did not forget his family." Reading the Bible in a different voice is to hear the truth of a God who "so loved the world"—not just one discrete segment of the world.

We also need to move beyond the modern craving to acquire more and more information for its own sake. We need a dynamic relationship with God's living Word like that of Jeremiah who said, "When your words came, I ate them; they were my joy and my heart's delight, for I bear your name, O LORD God Almighty" (Jeremiah 15:16).[3]

Is there a way to read Scripture so that it reaches and reshapes our hearts, minds, bodies and spirits? Is there a way to approach the Bible for transformation and not merely information? In answer to these questions, Wesley Kort recommends two ways to read the Bible postmodernly: First there is "centripetal reading" (the force that drives us into the text), and then there is "centrifugal reading" (the force that drives us out again).

Centripetal Reading: Going into the Text

Kort explains that to read the Bible as a sacred text involves "movement away from self and world." We have to leave our world—with all of its presuppositions, values, and prejudices—as we move into the biblical world. We have to deny self to go on the biblical journey. "[T]he reader, like the disciples, is enjoined to leave all behind and to follow, not simply to see what will happen or to draw moral and theological conclusions but also to die."[4] Only by laying aside the self—with its narrow mind-set—can we experience the real power of the Bible.

If the Bible is going to transform our lives, we must give up who we were before coming to the Scripture. The "old self" is an enemy of God's truth. It intrudes on our Bible reading, preventing us from seeing everything that is there and keeping us from being transformed by it. Thus we can read what the Bible says about taking care of the poor yet never help the poor, or we can know what the Bible says about showing reverence to God, yet never fear Him.

Practically speaking, how can we strip away the self when we read the Bible? Well, we might begin with the realization that the Scripture is *right* and we are *wrong*. This is the point Paul made in Romans 7:7-24. There he says things like "We know that the law is spiritual; but I am unspiritual, sold as a slave to sin" (verse 14) and "For in my inner being I delight in God's law; but I see another law at work in the members of my body, waging war against the law of my mind and making me a prisoner of the law of sin at work within my members" (verses 22-23). If we come to the Bible knowing that our thinking, attitudes, and behavior need to be corrected, and that an authentic reading of the Bible will take us to the end of ourselves, then we are prepared to read it with a view to being transformed by it.

When we step out of self and our world to enter the Bible, we discover people who were also called to leave their homes, families, and old selves to journey with God. Wesley Kort reminds us that Abraham was willing to "leave the security of his familiar home and to go to a place not only where he has never been but about which he knows nothing."[5] So we not only leave self behind when we step into the Bible, but there is further stripping away of self when we join the men and women of Scripture in their adventure with God.

We are not looking for new concepts to analyze or even specific commandments to obey. We are using our imaginations to put ourselves in the shoes (sandals) of biblical characters so we can feel in our own heart the call of God to them, what it meant and at what cost. Rather than learning new Bible lessons, we are experiencing the Bible's power.

Centripetal reading of Scripture is a process by which we undergo the transformation and renewal of our minds (Romans 12:2). Through this authentic engagement with Scripture, we surrender to God, who reshapes our lives, redefines our reality, and gives us a new name, which is to say, a new identity. Just as Abram became Abraham, so we become new men and women and our lives are placed on a new path with a new destination. According to Clark Pinnock, this is a reading of Scripture in which the word *inspiration* applies to both the "text *and* reader."[6]

When we read the Bible in this way, we are shaken out of our self-sufficiency, our pride, our false confidences. We no longer strut, but with Jacob we limp. When Jacob wrestled with God, he received more than a new name and a new identity. Richard Rorty expects an "inspired" reading of a text to leave a person either "enraptured or destabilized," affecting the reader's "conception of who she is, what she is good for, what she wants to do with herself: an encounter which has rearranged her priorities and purposes."[7] The further we sink into Scripture, the further it carries us away from our comfortable, self-centered lives and closer to the wisdom and will of God.

When my son Will was about eight years old, his Sunday-school teacher approached me after a service and said, "You know, teaching your son is quite a challenge. Whenever I begin a Bible story, he always says, 'Oh, I know that one,' and then he finishes the story for me."

Will, who is now twenty-four years old, has recently warmed my heart by coming to me with new insights from the Bible. He will say something like, "I had never seen this before. But look how profound it is!" He is rediscovering the Bible because he is now reading it the way a starving man would eat a loaf of bread. He feels the texture, tastes the flavors, and enjoys the aroma. And the Bible is changing his outlook, his affections, his life. He is entering the text and allowing it to wound and heal, humble and exalt, tear down and build up.

An authentic engagement with God's Word means that we are not trying to get through our ten chapters for the day. We are not merely trying to learn, but we are listening for God to speak to us. We are waiting for Him to search us, to know us, and to discover any wickedness hidden in our hearts.

One clarification needs to be made at this point. Though an authentic engagement with the Bible drives us out of our laziness and self-indulgence, it does not mean that we are looking for passages that make us feel inadequate, guilty, and worthless. We do not go to the Bible looking for confirmation of our inner belief that we are nothing but scum.

Because fundamentalist guilt and Roman Catholic guilt are so pervasive in our society, we have to distinguish between the way God speaks to us and the way we tend to condemn ourselves. God disciplines us in love (Hebrews 12:5-11), and He affirms us even as He corrects us. God's Word may take us out of the old self, but He also brings us into the new self "created to be like God in true righteousness and holiness" (Ephesians 4:24). If Scripture convicts us, it also contains a powerful "Well done" that affirms our dignity and worth in the sight of God.

Centrifugal Reading: Going Out of the Text

After delving deeply into the Scripture, there is a point where we turn around and emerge—as Jesus was driven into the wilderness and then "returned to Galilee in the power of the Spirit" (Luke 4:14). Centrifugal reading, Kort says, is a return to our world. After being immersed in the Bible, we return as different people, and our world appears to us in a new way—somehow invisibly infused with the kingdom of God.

Again, the limping Jacob, renamed Israel, is an example of how we emerge from the text. The new name means we no longer are defined by our old life or culture. We now are defined by God. Our encounter with God in His Word humbles us so that we are less surefooted in our dogmatism, arrogance, and prejudice. We now are able to understand what Paul meant when he said, "So, if you think you are standing firm, be careful that you don't fall!" (1 Corinthians 10:12). We actually serve God better when we are personally off balance (2 Corinthians 12:7-10). We reenter the world to minister to others, but we do so as changed people.

If God's Word is so powerful, why do we see so little transformation in the lives of people who supposedly are Bible experts? The answer lies in a parable of Jesus, in which He described a farmer planting seed, and the four types of soil on which the seed fell (Mark 4:3-20). Sometimes the words of Jesus never enter the heart of the person who reads or hears them. Other times, His words are not allowed to develop strong roots. Other times whatever life is produced by his words is choked out by worldly anxieties and ambitions. If the Bible is not radically changing the lives of Christians, it is not because the seed is no good but because there are problems with the soil.

In the book of Revelation, John was given a scroll from heaven and told to eat it. When he did, it tasted sweet in his mouth but turned bitter in his stomach (Revelation 10:8-10). Most Christians have had the sweet experience of Bible study or devotional reading, but less often have we had the agonizing experience of the Bible really working within us—working *against* us because of fundamental flaws in our character or behavior.

If we are going to be wounded by the Bible so God can heal us properly, if we are going to be the right kind of soil in which His Word takes root, then we are going to have to be very serious about our engagement with Scripture. In the words of Helmut Thielicke, "The Word of God demands a stretch of time in our day—even though it be a very modest one—in which it is our only companion. We can't bite off a simple 'text for the day' and swallow it in one lump while we have our hand on the doorknob. Such things are not digested; they are not assimilated into one's organism."[8] We must seriously devote ourselves to centripetal reading, which drives us deeply into the biblical text, before centrifugal reading drives us back out into the world as changed creatures.

Authentic Engagement with Other Believers

The world is not going to be changed by Christians who merely go to church. The nature of the church in postmodernity has to be that of a spiritual community that strives to go beyond the modern concern for correct doctrine and institutionalism. A spiritual community is not based on dogma but on relationship to God and to one another.

The postmodern church also will find that the little systems of biblical interpretation that separate one church from another are not as great as the big beliefs, such as the Nicene or Apostles' Creed, which tie all Christians together. Rather than define our little systems as orthodox, we will acknowledge that they are merely preferences, while the word *orthodox* will be retained for the primary doctrines of the Christian faith. Postmodern Christians will fight less and dialogue more, finding much to learn and borrow from other denominations to enhance their own symbols, devotion, and worship.

In 2 Corinthians 6:1, Paul referred to the Christians in Corinth as his "fellow workers," which translates the Greek word *sunergeo*. This word comes into English as *synergy* or *synergism*, which, according to the Funk and Wagnalls online dictionary, is "the interaction of elements that when combined produce a total effect that is greater than the sum of the individual elements, contributions, etc." The postmodern church will discover its synergism, its collective muscle.

The spiritual community is the body of Christ as described by Paul (Romans 12; 1 Corinthians 12; Ephesians 4). It is a collection of people who are committed to God, to His mission in the world, and to each other. But for the church to produce true synergism, its members must be personally and deeply involved in its life through mutual give and take, genuine relationship building, and ongoing devotion to God while maintaining its outward momentum toward the world. Individual members of the church community add strength to the whole, and the whole gives strength to the individual (1 Corinthians 12:7).

Even though the church is vitally important for promoting God's work in postmodern culture, churches may not be ready to function as spiritual communities. We have seen that postmodernity characteristically produces images detached from reality. Unfortunately, religious institutions can project the church "image" even when there is no real spiritual community. According to the Bible, when something exists in appearance but is without substance, it is considered either hypocrisy or idolatry.[9]

A church is not a true spiritual community if the intention of the minister and church leaders is to embed people in the "institution" through programs designed for that purpose. One church strategy popular with large or growing churches is to seize visitors as soon as they walk in the door and induct them into a series of classes with the intent of moving them into formal membership and deeper commitment to the institution. Of course, it is assumed that along the way they will make a genuine commitment to

Christ, discover their spiritual gifts, grow into ministry, and devote themselves to Christian service. But at the same time the critically important theme of church membership is implicitly, if not explicitly, stated every step of the way.

Churches that typically require a lot of maintenance to keep the institution going are large churches, churches that run a lot of programs, or churches weighted by tradition. In other words, the members must use their energy and money to serve the institution and its structures. They have less opportunity to serve each other face to face because there are so many committees to run, meetings to attend, and obligations to meet just to maintain the organization.

However, members of large churches can put their consciences at ease in the knowledge that as long as they support the church and its programs, the institution will take care of all those pesky problems such as foreign missions, feeding the hungry, providing shelter for the homeless, bringing meals to the sick, visiting prisoners, and so on. Somehow members can vicariously and anonymously accomplish all those tasks—for which Jesus said we will be judged (Matthew 25:31-46)—simply by putting money into the capable hands of the professional church staff.

Real community is a web of personal relationships built on deep trust and commitment. Spiritual communities do not need to organize small groups because they are either a small group or an environment in which small groups naturally form—as in the book of Acts, where more than five thousand believers living in Jerusalem "broke bread in their homes and ate together" in what we must assume were small groups (Acts 2:46).

I am doubtful that an effective spiritual community can grow much larger than three hundred members. When a church grows beyond three hundred, additional staff must be added (who also need to be led, reviewed, managed), which increases the financial burden as well as the bureaucracy of the institution. Beyond three hundred, something vital is lost among the members: intimacy and accountability. We no longer know everyone's name, nor can we stay abreast of all the latest events in everyone's life (whose parent passed away, whose sister had a baby, and so on). Large churches are still important, but the trade-offs are significant. We often sacrifice quality for quantity in regard to human relationships.

The danger of small churches, especially in postmodernity, is that they become ingrown, they lose their vision for lost humanity, and they lose their contact with the outside world. When we become isolated, we run a greater risk of becoming a cult. In fact, one thing the church must do to be effective in postmodernity is to break down the we/they division between church members and everyone else. "We" are not all good, and "they" are not all bad, as we sometimes come to believe.

The church is a *spiritual* community because of the Story it tells and retells whenever it gathers for worship. What makes the church a spiritual *community* is the multiple stories that unfold in the lives of the members and then are spread from one to another. We come to know God through the Story of Scripture, and we get to know one another through our personal stories. The postmodern church is about God's Story and our stories.

The Story told by the church is quite simply the whole Bible, which forms the theological foundation for the community. It is a Story of God's work in history, rescuing and reclaiming humans to Himself, and culminates in the Person of Jesus Christ. The many stories we tell are in some way derived from the one Story. All of our little stories converge in God's Story and are braided together by it. Every Christian, therefore, is a storyteller.[10]

When speakers lecture, their goal is to instruct or educate their audience. When people tell stories, they want to lead their audience to an experience. Stories evoke imagination, and imagination serves the goal of the storyteller by creating in the hearers an experience of what is told. If I *learn* that people are suffering from oppression and starvation in the Sudan, I may have empathy for their problem, but it is merely information. In contrast, if I *experience* their suffering, then I own it and I also own the feeling that I must do something for them.

In postmodernity, Christians must learn that no one can control the interpretation of Scripture. Many interpretations will be offered for a single text, texts are capable of multiple readings, and leaving the text open for other meanings allows the Holy Spirit to produce new applications for familiar passages. In fact, we cannot take control of the interpretation of Scripture because that is the role of the Holy Spirit who illumines and enlightens.

This is not to say that all interpretations are equal. The modern disciplines of biblical study still are vital for discerning the author's intent and how the original audience interpreted the text. Not all interpretations are created equal, yet all need to be heard, considered, and sifted through for those that do contain a true sense of God's message to human hearts. After all, who could have foreseen that Jeremiah's prophecy about Rachel weeping for her children would find fulfillment in the massacre of the innocents of Bethlehem? (Jeremiah 31:15-17; Matthew 2:18).

Both our preachers and church members must be storytellers in the postmodern church. In the same way that centripetal reading increases our engagement with Scripture, so storytelling increases our engagement with God's presence in worship. The preacher must be able to help people see, hear, and perceive the claims of the gospel (Mark 8:17-21). For example, Paul could say to the Galatians, "Before your very eyes Jesus Christ was clearly portrayed as crucified." He reminded them they had received the Spirit by "believing what you heard" (Galatians 3:1-2). John, whose gospel proves he was a gifted storyteller, said:

> That which was from the beginning, which we have heard,
> which we have seen with our eyes, which we have looked at and

our hands have touched—this we proclaim concerning the
Word of life. The life appeared; we have seen it and testify to it,
and we proclaim to you the eternal life, which was with the
Father and has appeared to us. We proclaim to you what we
have seen and heard, so that you also may have fellowship with
us. And our fellowship is with the Father and with his Son, Jesus
Christ. (1 John 1:1-3)

One scholar has suggested on the basis of this passage that every sermon
should give the hearers something to look at, something to hear, and something to handle.

The Metanarrative Challenge

Stories abound in our time. Almost every television commercial tells a story
with sights and sounds. Even many print ads tell stories. The challenge we
face is postmodernism's suspicion or skepticism of metanarratives, grand or
universal stories. How are we to face this challenge?

We must remember that within postmodernity every subculture and
tribe is allowed its own narrative, its own sacred text. Believers can legitimately present the Bible to the world as the Christian narrative. In this way
the church is able to get its foot in the door of public discourse. If we can
avoid talking like dictators—as though everyone had to adopt our view of
reality—and speak instead of "the way Christians believe," people will be
more inclined to hear what we have to say. Postmodernists find absolute
language threatening, dubious, and offensive.

At the same time, the church must discourage people, within and without, from treating God's Story as any other story. God's Story, according to
Christian belief, is the grand narrative in a time when no story is considered
superior and no grand narrative is supposed to exist, and this is how it must

189

be presented. In telling God's Story, the church enables both its members and the world outside to experience its ultimacy and truth, finding in it the Story that transcends and locates all other stories.

Authentic Engagement with Popular Culture

A few years ago, a religion editor for the *Orange County Register* asked if I would drive up to Hollywood with him to see Martin Scorcese's film *Last Temptation of Christ*. The editor wanted to include my response to the movie in his column. I agreed to go with him and another minister, but when we arrived at the theater there were no more seats, so we missed the movie.

Last Temptation had been released a few days earlier, so it was rapidly becoming "old news." Nevertheless, there was a crowd of angry Christians toting signs and yelling at passersby. A large man in a slick, dark suit walked past me, carrying an oversized Bible and being trailed by a small band of followers. He seemed to be looking for someone. As he passed, I could not help but notice that his face was thick with pancake makeup. He had come prepared for the television cameras.

The church has not put its best foot forward when attempting to enter popular culture. On the one hand, there are believers who live in isolation from popular culture and enter it only to criticize, fight, and condemn it. On the other hand, there are believers so enmeshed and enamored with popular culture that they lose their spiritual distinctiveness. And let's be honest about Christian television programming, which, if not for the support of loyal partners, would die off because of its irrelevance.

The popular culture of postmodernity is not adverse to blatant Christian symbols and themes. A current spate of movies feature and even exploit Christian tradition and doctrine in their plots. Rather than complain that

Hollywood never is able to get the story straight (meaning perfectly biblical), we might ask once in a while, "What did they get right?" The answers to this question may be exactly the place where we can introduce the gospel.

Paul, again, serves as a good example of borrowing from mainstream culture to create a bridge for the gospel. His actions in Athens are instructive for Christians who want to find inroads into popular culture.

> While Paul was waiting for them in Athens, he was greatly distressed to see that the city was full of idols. So he reasoned in the synagogue with the Jews and the God-fearing Greeks, as well as in the marketplace day by day with those who happened to be there....
>
> Paul then stood up in the meeting of the Areopagus and said: "Men of Athens! I see that in every way you are very religious. For as I walked around and looked carefully at your objects of worship, I even found an altar with this inscription: TO AN UNKNOWN GOD. Now what you worship as something unknown I am going to proclaim to you." (Acts 17:16-17,22-23)

Paul's experience in Athens—at one time the intellectual capital of the world—provides a good model for engaging culture. Paul spoke in the synagogue, but also in the marketplace. He knew his audience in the synagogue would be "Jews and God-fearing Greeks," but he didn't stop there. He wanted to communicate with those people of Athens who had no connection with the God of Israel, so he hit the streets.

We cannot influence popular culture or speak to its issues, needs, and sins unless we enter it and observe it. For a long time there have been Christians who have felt that any contact with non-Christians and their entertainment and amusements is contaminating, compromising, and weakens one's commitment to God. However, the truth is that there is no place in popular culture a Christian cannot enter provided we know who we are, we do not forget our mission, and we refuse to indulge in anything prohibited by Scripture.

Paul not only entered the marketplace, but he also "looked carefully" at the Athenian objects of devotion. Perhaps some of their statues or shrines would have been blasphemous or lewd by Christian standards, and perhaps that had something to do with the fact that he was "greatly distressed" at what he saw. But this was the culture of the people he wanted to win, so he studied their objects of worship in order to know how to introduce the gospel to them.

What else can we learn from Paul's visit to Athens that will help us establish a spiritual beachhead in popular culture?

First, Find Points of Entry

Christian evangelists have not been known for their subtlety. They tend to barge in on people and cram religion down their throats regardless of whether anyone wants to listen. Paul, however, looked for a place within the culture where the truth of the gospel might match the context of the people's lives. He found that point of entry at a shrine dedicated to the Unknown God. The fact that such a God "does not live in temples built by hands" is another point of entry (Acts 17:24).

Many times a particular television program, movie, or current event will be so significant that everyone is talking about it the next day around the factory, office, or school. If Christians are able to join those discussions, not bashing Hollywood for churning out trash but genuinely contributing perceptive insights, then we can plant seeds of truth in other people's minds. But in order to find points of entry, we must engage in cultural activities not only for entertainment but also with an alertness to the plot, significant themes, and crucial statements made within the context of the event.

Second, Find Sites Where God Is Already at Work

Paul found within Greek poetry a statement that paralleled the truth of Scripture, that we are God's offspring (Acts 17:28). Paul told the people of Lystra that though God allowed the nations to go their own way, He had "not left himself without testimony," but He gave witness to His kindness to humans through the blessings of nature (Acts 14:16-17). Paul found many sites in pagan cultures where God was at work before he arrived, and he capitalized on the work God had started.

We do not have to take God into popular culture since He is already there, giving people impressions, revealing shades of His truth, and leaving His fingerprints. If we can discover those sites where He already is at work, then we can speak to our culture in terms they can understand.

Third, Find People Who Are Thinking Spiritually

Paul talked to the Athenians about their spiritual beliefs without being condescending or critical. He wove themes from their philosophy and religion into his message, correcting some of their wrong notions and utilizing what they had right. Their spiritual thinking, as immature as it may have been, provided him with an avenue to introduce Christian ideas by relating them to ideas the Athenians already accepted.

There are writers who are doing a good job of communicating spiritual themes to popular culture. Few of them are ministers. Some are psychologists, others are journalists, others are rabbis, and some are a new breed of Eastern guru. Certainly there is much misinformation, distortion, and nonsense (*A Course in Miracles*, *The Celestine Prophecy*, and *Conversations with God* come to mind). But we need to know, and respect, the spiritual sensitivities of popular culture to help us find ways to address the Christian themes we would like to see promoted.

When we look into the spiritual thinking of popular culture, we need to ask these questions: What does this reveal about the spiritual climate of the culture? What does it reveal about their perceptions of God and the spiritual life? What does it say, if anything, about Christian truths such as redemption? Knowing the spiritual mood of popular culture helps us frame our message in ways that people already find acceptable. We do not need to alter the truth but to repackage it.

After spending twenty years away from the church, Kathleen Norris felt compelled to return. But as soon as she crossed the threshold, she was bombarded with what she called the "scary words" of the Christian faith, "Words like 'Antichrist,' 'blood,' 'dogma,' 'revelation.'" She realized that in order to truly embrace the church she was going to have to rebuild her religious vocabulary. But unlike the modern habit of going to a Bible dictionary to discover the meaning of these words, Norris set about to experience their meaning in life situations. The result of this pursuit is a volume entitled *Amazing Grace: A Vocabulary of Faith.*

Norris has done an excellent job of discerning the spiritual mood of our culture and introducing Christian truth in a way that people find interesting. She has made the language of Christian faith accessible to a wide audience. But she was wise enough to avoid writing a dictionary, which would have been a typically modern approach to her project. Instead, she says, "I have compiled this 'lexicon' in the firm conviction that human beings are essentially storytelling bipeds, and that dictionary definitions of potent religious words, while useful in understanding one's religious heritage, are of far less importance than the lived experience of them within that tradition."[11]

Fourth, Find Issues That Are Addressed by Scripture

We are not looking for the sins of society so that we can bash them. Instead we are looking for some of the missing pieces. There is no culture that contains all the necessary elements to keep all of its members perfectly satisfied.

There are questions and needs that only God can resolve. If we can find clear spiritual wisdom in the Bible for practical problems of life, we can show people that God is aware of their needs and has provided solutions.

Even after making our best efforts to engage with popular culture, we know that not everyone will say yes to God. Paul received a mixed response from his Athenian audience; "some of them sneered," others wanted to hear more, while a "few men became followers of Paul and believed" (Acts 17:32,34). We are not responsible for how people react; we are only responsible to get the truth to them in ways they can understand. If people turn away, it should not be because we have been obnoxious, unpleasant, unintelligible, or have in some way misrepresented God's truth.

Living from the Heart

As followers of the Lord, who was accused of socializing with sinners, we need to reconsider our network of friends. Some Christians have followed the pattern of cults and removed themselves from their former friends and alienated their families. We need to recover the relational way that Jesus Christ communicated His love, compassion, and generosity to other people.

Sometimes I am approached by a member of my church who wants to take me out to lunch to get to know me. It is only after we are seated that I discover the real reason we are dining together: I need life insurance. When this happens I feel tricked, deceived, violated.

Authentic engagement with nonbelievers means that we are willing to build relationships with them, get to know them and become known by them. Sometimes it is appropriate to share the message of salvation when we first meet a person, but other times people need to know our integrity, righteousness, and love for them before we tell the Story. The message communicated by your life and experience is more important in post-modernity than the message in words.

In modernity Christians learned how to monologue eloquently. Now we must learn how to dialogue. The pluralism of postmodernity requires us to listen at least as much as we speak. If all we do is preach at people, they will soon shut us off. If we show little regard for what they have to say, why should they regard what we have to say?

For the same reason, we will have to live our faith more in the style of Jesus Christ. Televangelists caught in scandals, television preachers who live lavish lifestyles while shedding tears for more funds, or Christian celebrities who make Scripture sound ridiculous have little impact on popular culture other than providing caricatures for parody or comic relief. But no one laughed at Mother Teresa.

Postmodernists want to *see* Christianity. They are not interested in reading a book. They do not require lengthy apologetic lectures. They simply want to see a real, honest-to-goodness Christian, someone who truly follows the merciful, compassionate, healing example of Jesus Christ.

For that reason, we must try to show kindness to everyone. If we demean flight attendants, our servers in restaurants, or the checker at the grocery store, we are speaking volumes to the postmodern mind. We need to apply personally what Paul told Timothy, that "The goal of this command is love, which comes from a pure heart and a good conscience and a sincere faith" (1 Timothy 1:5). In other words, we have to become the men and women whom others would like to have for friends.

To influence our world for God, we must speak, act, think, and live from our hearts. We were able to operate out of our minds in modernity, but information has become cheap and not altogether reliable. People who are true are now regarded more highly than people who are knowledgeable. We can hire the knowledgeable people, but we love the true people.

True Religion

I was in a hospital a few years ago, visiting a man who had suffered a stroke. Though he was normally an outgoing, friendly type of person, he and his wife stayed mostly on the periphery of our church. That day in the hospital we talked about his condition and recovery. When his nurse entered the room, he beamed a big smile and introduced me as his pastor. Then he added, "This man's going to change religion!"

What he meant was that religion was no longer going to be that dreary, miserable institution that everyone runs from. No longer would religion have to be boring yet demanding, always standing with its hand out as if you could never give enough. He meant that religion was going to become something beautiful, desirable, healthy, and maybe even fun at times.

A changed religion could possibly change the world. The opportunity is on our doorstep. We have not seen the church in a historical situation so suited for renewal and improvement since the time of the Reformation. Postmodernity is opening its doors to spirituality, and the spiritual leaders— of whatever stripe or belief—who are not afraid of popular culture will be the first to enter. Do we have to let the kooks get there first? Do we have to drag our feet until the window of opportunity has once again closed?

Pioneers? Explorers? Yes, the church needs men and women who are not afraid of leaving the security of the past, people who will hoist their mainsail and head into the uncharted waters of the future, people who believe that God is always on the horizon. The church needs adventurers who ask nothing for their journey besides the North Star of Scripture to guide them, the wind of the Spirit to propel them, and an occasional spray in their face to refresh them. And with people of this mettle, God can build a church that will rock the postmodern world.

Notes

Postmodernism is a complicated subject that, in philosophical and academic circles, includes such themes as semiotics, philology, and literary criticism. I did not want to burden this book with the foundation of postmodern thought, which we may safely leave underground and out of sight. But I felt that perhaps a few issues needed fuller explanations. So I have provided some background information in the following notes for those who are interested in digging a little deeper. Also included is bibliographic data on the books I cited in the text.

I assume that most readers will not be interested in this technical information, but a few may appreciate the opportunity to expand their own research into postmodernism, and I hope these notes will be useful for that purpose. They contain no information that is vital to understanding the text of this book, so read them or skip them according to your own interest level and needs.

Introduction

1. Regarding the irrelevance of an author in contemporary literature, what else would you expect to happen when a text is defined as "a machine conceived in order to elicit interpretations," in the words of Umberto Eco in *Interpretation and Overinterpretation* (New York: Cambridge University Press, 1992, p. 85)? The postmodern view of a text (defined broadly as a book, screenplay, or even an event) is that it stands independent of its author.

   In Eco's view, once a text is published, it belongs to the readers, and they are likely to make something out of it that the author never intended. Sometimes the "intention of the text" (not necessarily the author's intention) is used to argue against "overinterpretation" (reading too much into a text), but in Eco's words, "the intention of the empirical author has been totally disregarded." His strategy of textual interpretation "makes the notion of an empirical author's intention radically useless. We have to respect the text, not the author as person so-and-so."

Nevertheless, Eco concedes cases in which the "empirical author" is relevant in everyday communication when one person is trying to express a subjective feeling to another, or when authors interact with other readers of their text in looking for interpretations while avoiding overinterpretations (pp. 65-6). But for the most part, Eco's role for the empirical author is clear: "I have introduced the empirical author in this game only in order to stress his irrelevance and to reassert the rights of the text" (p. 84).

Stanley Fish does an excellent job of covering this ground in his book of essays *Is There a Text in This Class? The Authority of Interpretive Communities* (Cambridge: Harvard University Press, 1980).

2. Suzanna Sherry, interview by Ken Meyers; July/August 1998, Mars Hill Tapes, cassette tape: "A bimonthly audio magazine of contemporary culture & Christian conviction," Volume 33. Mars Hill Audio, P.O. Box 1527 Charlottesville, VA 22902-1527. The interview with Sherry centered on the book she coauthored with Daniel Farber, *Beyond All Reason: The Radical Assault on Truth in American Law.*

3. Cal Thomas and Ed Dobson, *Blinded by Might: Can the Religious Right Save America?* (Grand Rapids, Mich.: Zondervan Publishing House, 1999), 42-3.

4. Cal Thomas and Ed Dobson, *Blinded by Might*, 23.

5. Paul Weyrich, "A Moral Minority: An open letter to conservatives by Paul Weyrich," Free Congress Research and Education Foundation, 717 Second Street, NE, Washington, D.C. Free Congress Online, freecongress.org, February 16, 1999.

6. Lynne Cheney, *Telling the Truth: Why Our Culture and Our Country Have Stopped Making Sense—and What We Can Do About It* (New York: Simon & Schuster, 1995), 96-7.

7. I have chosen not to distinguish cultural postmodernism from postmodernity or postmodernism. I might be in danger of mixing discrete ideas, but the term *postmodern* is large enough to subsume all of the various categories and nuances, especially in its sociological context.

   Jean-François Lyotard—whose work, *The Postmodern Condition* (Minneapolis: University of Minnesota Press, 1997), put the term *postmodern* on the intellectual map—referred to postmodernism in popular culture as "eclecticism," which he termed the "degree zero of contemporary general culture" (p. 79). Though Lyotard criticized eclecticism for being money-driven "in the absence of aesthetic criteria" and "taste," it is important to understand this type of postmodern culture for the purposes of Christian mission. After all, popular culture is where we encounter and experience postmodernity most frequently.

   Some scholars question whether the changes taking place in the world really can be described as a new era, different from modernity, or merely the next stage of modernity. But something is happening to our world, and we are moving away from reality as defined by the modern era. "Many people fervently hope that postmodernism—whatever they mean by it—will go away," observes Walter Anderson. He adds: "Postmodernisms will come and go, but postmodernity—the postmodern condition—will still be here. It is a major transition in human history, a time of rebuilding all the foundations of civilization, and the world is going to be occupied with it for a long time to come. And, although it touches different people in vastly different ways, it is happening to us all" (Walter Anderson, *The Truth About the Truth: De-confusing and Re-constructing the Postmodern World*, New York: Tarcher/Putnam, 1995, pp. 7-8).

For our purposes, the word *postmodern* will be used in two contexts: first, in reference to a great historical transition from modernity into postmodernity; and second, to an influence of thought that is present in a variety of disciplines that often are called *postmodern* (art, literature, political theory, popular culture, and so forth). *Postmodern* may not be the best word to describe the new era that is dawning, but for now it is "a makeshift word we use until we have decided what to name the baby," in the words of Walter Anderson (p. 3).

Chapter 1

1. Daniel Yankelovich, *New Rules* (New York: Random House, 1981), xiv.

2. Alvin Toffler, *Powershift* (New York: Bantam Books, 1990), xix.

3. In discussions regarding the nature of reality, themes from cultural anthropology prove helpful, and especially Chuck Kraft's *Christianity and Culture* (Maryknoll, N. Y.: Orbis, 1981). Reality for premodern people was fairly simple. The real world outside was identical to their perception of it. Their words could describe and embody what was real. (This view is sometimes referred to as "naive realism.")

    Modern thinkers, however, challenged that concept of reality and created a gap between our internal picture of reality and the external world of objects. When René Descartes asked how he could be certain his idea of the world accurately corresponded to the real world, he created a fracture between perception and reality. Descartes made the distinction between the world in his head and the world outside as it really existed.

    Before the modern age, people assumed there was a connection between their world and their experience of it. According to Ted Peters, Descartes's "subject-object split" eventually led to the "present widespread standard for truth—that is, the assumption that truth must be objective.... Genuine knowledge is impersonal" (*God—the World's Future*, Minneapolis: Fortress, 1992, p. 10). Humans were venturing on a philosophical path unknown to their predecessors, which eventually led them to a new worldview. Reality was morphing.

The work of eighteenth-century philosopher David Hume was important because his "radical empiricism" promoted the skepticism that has marked the modern age. He argued that the only thing humans can really be sure of is their perceptions, which he divided into impressions (sense experience and emotions) and ideas (which are borrowed from our impressions; mental "copies" of our impressions). He claimed it was impossible to prove that there is any substance to the external world since all we experience is our perceptions of objects and not the actual objects themselves.

W. T. Jones, in *A History of Western Philosophy*, describes Hume's view: "The mind is a kind of theater, where several perceptions successively make their appearance; pass, re-pass, glide away, and mingle in an infinite variety of postures and situations" (New York: Harcourt, Brace & World, 1952, p. 770). Descartes believed he could prove the existence of the world and eventually the existence of God, based first of all on his own existence and then using mathematics to prove the rest. Hume, however, claimed it was impossible to prove the existence of God. His skepticism set the mood for philosophy throughout the entire modern period.

Eventually the force of Hume's thought permeated almost every academic institution and finally filtered down into general culture. Through the influence of Hume and Immanuel Kant, who was inspired by Hume, philosophers despaired of being able to prove the existence of God by reason or sense experience.

4. Douglas Coupland, *Generation X: Tales for an Accelerated Generation* (New York: St. Martin's Press, 1991), 8.

5. Walter Truett Anderson, *Reality Isn't What It Used to Be* (San Francisco: Harper Collins, 1990), 27.

6. For a comprehensive discussion of the ramifications of the birth of the modern era, see Paul Johnson, *The Birth of the Modern* (New York: Harper Collins, 1991).

7. Herbert Kohl, *From Archetype to Zeitgeist: Powerful Ideas for Powerful Thinking* (Boston: Little, Brown, 1992), 62.

8. Stanley Grenz delineates the Enlightenment Principles, which help to clarify the mood of the early modern period. First, "reason," which would unlock the laws of nature and enable humans to transform the world. Second, "nature," in the sense of natural order or the nature of a thing, which gave the world its coherence and made it understandable. There were not only natural laws but even the possibility of a "natural theology." Third, "autonomy," which referred to the responsibility humans had to make wise decisions now that human reason had replaced external authorities for truth and action. Fourth, "harmony," which reigned in the universe in spite of the diversity of its parts. Humans needed to find the proper balance between their lives and the "harmony of the cosmos." Finally, "progress," which was an inevitable feature of the human quest for knowledge through reason. One day humans would know all there was to know about the universe and would create a utopia where they would live in happiness and freedom. (Stanley Grenz and Roger Olson, *Twentieth Century Theology: God and the World in a Transitional Age,* Downers Grove, Ill.: InterVarsity, 1992, pp. 20-2. Stanley Grenz, *A Primer on Postmodernism,* Grand Rapids: Eerdmans, 1996, pp. 67-71).

9. Robert Solomon, *Continental Philosophy Since 1750: The Rise and Fall of the Self* (New York: Oxford University Press, 1988), 9.

10. If the proper way to scientifically study a subject is value-neutral, then moral categories are removed from the hard sciences. Modern science invented the myth of an objective observer who could stand outside a field of research, run experiments, note results, and yet not be personally involved in the subject under investigation. Scientists had to be dispassionate, that is, emotionally disconnected from their experiments. Modern science was supposed to be amoral so its research would not be contaminated by personal bias. The idea of God having a determining influence in the universe also was ruled out by scientists who were trying to answer the riddles of nature completely on their own.

11. Most scholars give René Descartes at least partial credit for the development of this marked individualism of modernity. Descartes wanted to produce a philosophy that was built on absolute certainty. To do so, according to Ed Miller in *Questions that Matter* (New York: McGraw-Hill, 1984), Descartes began by doubting "anything and everything that was doubtable, in hopes of discovering something, even one thing, that was not doubtable, something certain, something unshakable, some indubitable truth that might serve as a secure foundation of his philosophy" (p. 101). The philosopher concluded that the one thing he could know for certain was that he was a thinking being. In the words of Robert Solomon: "Descartes's epochal change in philosophy was very much a move towards subjectivity and the self, and the method of the empiricists—however opposed to Descartes—strengthened the emphases on experience and introspective reflection, on the nature of the identity of the self, and on the importance of the first-person standpoint. Indeed, there is no question but that Descartes, 'the father of modern philosophy,' was also the founder of the modern philosophical obsession with the self as the locus and arbiter of knowledge" (*Continental Philosophy Since 1750*, New York: Oxford University Press, 1988, p. 5).

12. W. T. Jones, *A History of Western Philosophy* (New York: Harcourt, Brace & World, 1952), 69.

13. Harvey Cox, *The Secular City* (New York: Macmillan, 1978), 12.

14. Stanley Grenz's and Roger Olson's work *Twentieth Century Theology* (Downers Grove, Ill.: InterVarsity, 1992) is an invaluable guide to the important theological movements of the twentieth century. They point out: "Like Hume's, Kant's theory of knowing placed great limits on the ability of thinkers to argue from sense experience to transcendent realities, such as God, the immortal soul and human freedom. The position Kant developed in the *Critique of Pure Reason* meant that any reality that lies beyond space and time cannot be known through the scientific enterprise, because science is based on sense experience" (p. 27).

    For a philosophical refutation of the philosophical dismissal of God, I would highly recommend Brian D. Ingraffia's *Postmodern Theory and Biblical Theology* (New York: Cambridge University Press, 1995). His argument (admittedly oversimplified here) is that the god that Nietzsche declared to be dead and whose existence neither modern science nor modern philosophy could prove was not the God of biblical revelation but the god of ontotheology. Therefore, the weakness of the rejection of God of some postmodern writers is also the fact that the god they deconstruct is the god of onto-theology.

Chapter 2

1. Commenting on the effect photography had on developments in art, Steven Connor observes, "Indeed, one may say that it was partly in reaction to the widespread dissemination of photographic technology that modern painting was forced to turn from representation into the abstract interrogation of its

own forms and conditions." (*Postmodern Culture: An Introduction to Theories of the Contemporary,* Oxford, U.K.: Blackwell Publishers, 1997, p. 105.)

2. Modern art is modern not only because it broke away from the classical tradition of representation, but also because it borrowed from both the science and philosophy of modernity to produce new styles. Artists concerned about the integrity of their work "struggled to penetrate the 'deeper' reality, to represent what has been made invisible for the convention-bound eye." So where did they turn for help? According to Zygmunt Bauman, in *Intimations of Postmodernity* (New York: Routledge, 1994), "To attain such 'better,' correct, true representation, they sought the guidance of science: that recognized authority on what reality is really like. Thus the impressionists took inspiration (and legitimation for their practices) from optics, cubists from the relativity theory, surrealists from psychoanalysis" (p. 28). Modernity provided themes and means for the new forms of painting.

3. About fifteen years ago I attempted to produce a surreal painting of a biblical theme over an Israeli-type landscape. I rarely had more than a couple of hours at a time to sit at my easel, but after many mistakes and much learning, my work gradually took shape. All along I mixed and tested the acrylic paint colors on a small canvas by my palate. When several months passed without my being able to work on my masterpiece (which even my children would have been embarrassed to sign), I stored it away in the garage. About the same time, someone saw the colorful scrap of canvas I had used for mixing the colors and asked me if it was available to frame.

4. Charles Jenks, quoted in Richard Appiganesi, *Introducing Postmodernism* (New York: Totem Books, 1995), 3.

5. Jean-François Lyotard, *The Postmodern Condition: A Report on Knowledge* (Minneapolis: University of Minnesota Press, 1997), 81.

6. What happens to a painting that is disconnected from the real world or any reality outside the canvas? The painting itself becomes the only "reality." In *Simulacra and Simulation* (Ann Arbor: University of Michigan Press, 1999), the French postmodern philosopher Jean Baudrillard enumerates the four phases in which an image goes from being a representation to becoming a simulacrum (a copy of a copy for which there is no original):

it is the reflection of a profound reality;

it masks and denatures a profound reality;

it masks the *absence* of a profound reality;

it has no relation to any reality whatsoever—it is its own pure simulacrum (p. 6).

In *The Image* (New York: Random House, 1992), Daniel Boorstin introduced the concept of "pseudo-events." Boorstin's brilliance is revealed in the last thirty years of world history and cultural progress, in which the visible distinction between sham and reality is difficult to assess because the "edges of reality" are blurred in contemporary culture. Boorstin explains: "The pseudo-events which flood our consciousness are neither true nor false in the old familiar senses. The very same advances which have made them possible have also made the images—however planned, contrived, or distorted—more vivid, more attractive, more impressive, and more persuasive than reality itself" (p. 36).

When it comes to famous people—"the human pseudo-event"—we must redefine celebrity to mean "a person who is known for his well-knownness." Boorstin is concerned about the loss of reality in popular culture. In contrast, Baudrillard celebrates that loss of reality. The simulated event and the real event are so confused, he says, that "it is *now impossible to isolate the process of the real,* or to prove the real" (*Simulacra and Simulation,* p. 21). All that is left is the *image.*

7. Zygmunt Bauman, *Intimations of Postmodernity* (New York: Routledge, 1994), 30.

8. Stanley J. Grenz, *A Primer on Postmodernism* (Grand Rapids: Eerdmans, 1996), 26.

9. Herbert Kohl, *From Archetype to Zeitgeist: Powerful Ideas for Powerful Thinking* (Boston: Little, Brown, 1992), 127.

10. Diogenes Allen, *Christian Belief in a Postmodern World: The Full Wealth of Conviction* (Louisville, Ky.: Westminster John Knox Press, 1989).

11. Ted Peters, *God—The World's Future: Systematic Theology for a Postmodern Era* (Minneapolis: Fortress Press, 1992), 6-7.

12. Allen, *Christian Belief in a Postmodern World*, 3.

13. Patrick Glynn, *God: The Evidence: The Reconciliation of Faith and Reason in a Postsecular World* (Rocklin, Calif.: Prima Publishing, 1997), 40.

14. Abraham Maslow, *Religions, Values, and Peak-Experiences* (New York: Penguin, 1977), 9-10.

15. Steven Weinberg, *Dreams of a Final Theory* (New York: Pantheon Books, 1992), 250.

16. John Eccles, "Science Can't Explain 'Who Am I? Why Am I Here?'" *U. S. News & World Report,* 10 December 1984, 80.

17. Christopher Lasch, *The True and Only Heaven: Progress and Its Critics* (New York: W. W. Norton, 1991), 168.

18. Paul Johnson, *The Birth of the Modern* (New York: Harper Collins, 1991), 545.

19. Ray Anderson, *The Soul of Ministry* (Louisville, Ky.: Westminster John Knox Press, 1997), 120-2.

Chapter 3

1. For an interesting look at the world of postmodernism, check out Jim Powell's brief but excellent analysis of *Blade Runner* in his comic book *Postmodernism for Beginners* (New York: Writers and Readers Publishing, 1998, pp. 122-30). He draws attention to the many "significant Postmodern elements" in the movie and demonstrates how it gave rise to the cyberpunk movement in science fiction and computer hacking. He apparently borrowed some of his ideas from David Harvey's analysis in *The Condition of Postmodernity* (United Kingdom: Blackwell, 1995, pp. 308-23).

2. Postmodernity is ambivalent about history. Unlike modernity, postmodernity is not an attempt to break with the past but selectively visits historical texts and creates for them new contexts to produce new meanings. According to David Harvey, history supplies postmodernists with a vast archive of images that may be brought out and assembled in any way one desires—it has "an incredible ability to plunder history and absorb whatever it finds there as some aspect of the present." He observes, "Through films, television, books, and the like, history and past experience are turned into a seemingly vast archive 'instantly retrievable and capable of being consumed over and over again at the push of a button.'… The postmodern penchant for jumbling together all manner of references to past styles is one of its more pervasive characteristics" (*The Condition of Postmodernity: An Enquiry into the Origins of Cultural Change*, United Kingdom, Blackwell Publishers, 1995, pp. 62-3).

3. Dennis McCallum, ed., *The Death of Truth: What's Wrong with Multiculturalism, the Rejection of Reason, and the New Postmodern Diversity* (Minneapolis: Bethany, 1996), 135.

4. Pauline Rosenau, *Post-Modernism and the Social Sciences: Insights, Inroads, and Intrusions* (Princeton, N.J.: Princeton University Press, 1992), 63,65.

5. In postmodern culture there are many ways to read and write history. According to postmodern theory, classical history favored white males and intensified their power in social structures by selectively including and excluding people and events that would yield a more egalitarian understanding of the development of society. One of the identifying features of postmodernity is the reinterpretation of history. New histories must be written, not to create a balance of power—which is neither possible nor desirable according to most postmodern thinkers—but to tip the scales in favor of those who have been marginalized, disenfranchised, and oppressed.

Justification for revising history (rereading history from a slanted perspective that privileges a minority voice) is found in the development of a postmodern theme that has its roots in Nietzsche's frequently cited statement that there are no facts, only interpretations. Again, reality disappears, and all we are left with is a simulacrum (a copy of a copy for which there is no original).

Revisionists are less concerned with the broad sociological trends (geopolitical, economic, etc.) that propelled historical events and more concerned with the case they want to make for a particular minority.

6. Rosenau, *Post-Modernism and the Social Sciences*, 77.

7. Stephen Grunlan and Marvin Mayers, *Cultural Anthropology: A Christian Perspective* (Grand Rapids: Zondervan, 1979), 26.

8. Paul Hiebert, *Cultural Anthropology* (Grand Rapids: Baker, 1983), 38-9.

9. Pauline Rosenau provides one of the clearest analyses of the role of the author in *Post-Modernism and the Social Sciences: Insights, Inroads, and Intrusions* (Princeton, N. J.: Princeton University Press, 1992, pp. 25-41). Her book is one of the most helpful in understanding the broad strands of postmodernism and its diverse representations.

10. Walter Truett Anderson, *Reality Isn't What It Used to Be* (San Francisco: Harper Collins, 1990), 9.

11. Norbert Schedler, ed., "Protean Man," *Philosophy of Religion: Contemporary Perspectives* (New York: Macmillan, 1974), 11.

Chapter 4

1. "And a believer, after all, is a lover; as a matter of fact, when it comes to enthusiasm, the most rapturous lover of all lovers is but a stripling compared with a believer." Those are the words of Søren Kierkegaard in *The Sickness unto Death* (Princeton, N.J.: Princeton University Press, 1980, p. 103). Modernity, with its attempt to reduce everything to rational propositions, tended to suck the mystery out of religious belief. Kierkegaard took to task ministers who felt it necessary to delineate the "the three reasons" for spiritual values such as love or prayer, "because praying has become so cheap that in order to raise its prestige a little three reasons have to be adduced." For example, regarding the preacher who attempts to prove "with three reasons that to pray is a bliss that 'passes all understanding,'" Kierkegaard writes: "What a priceless anticlimax—that something that passes all understanding—is proved by three reasons, which, if they do anything at all, presumably do not pass all understanding and, quite the contrary, inevitably make it obvious to the understanding that this bliss by no means passes all understanding, for 'reasons,' after all, lie in the realm of the understanding" (p. 103).

I suspect the self-help preaching of megachurch pastors will not have a long shelf life in the twenty-first century. It may be that the people who are flocking to them are desperate to hear (and trust) a voice of certainty and authority in a shaky and unstable world. But sooner or later almost everyone is going to be able to see through the "Ten Steps to a Perfect Marriage," "The Three Keys to Raising Godly Kids," "The Seven Secrets of Happiness." The complexities of human personalities cannot be broken down into discrete, workable units that easily. Bottom line: The "ten steps" and "seven secrets" and "twelve principles of success" are not universal—they don't work for everyone—and my guess is that it will get harder and harder to find someone for whom they do work.

Nevertheless, authoritarian preachers may still find large audiences because many people, panicked over changes in the world, will long for a dogmatism that assures them the world is predictable and life's troubles can be handled with quick fixes and simplistic solutions. Fundamentalisms of various kinds are likely to proliferate as each individual unit in society stakes its claim in popular culture and strives to be heard.

On the other hand, I wonder if the word *success*—a pervasive boomer theme and favorite of many self-help preachers—will have as much currency in the near future. Some people think churches need to redefine success, but my feeling is that success—as defined by acquisition of members, resources, popularity, and wealth—will be dropped from the church's vocabulary.

2. Alex Dominguez, Associated Press report, June 23, 1999.

3. A technical name has been given to writing history in this way: palimpsest history. The word *palimpsest* refers to a document in which one message has been poorly erased and another message written over it so that much of what was first written shows through. So two overlapping but different messages appear simultaneously. In historical novels, the two entities that overlap—whether nations, periods, events, or characters—are the fictional and non-fictional. See Christine Brooke-Rose's "Palimpsest History" in Umberto Eco's *Interpretation and Overinterpretation* (New York: Cambridge University Press, 1996, pp. 125-38).

4. Terry Eagleton, *The Illusions of Postmodernism* (Malden, Mass.: Blackwell Publishers, 1997), 45.

5. Steven Connor, *Postmodern Culture: An Introduction to Theories of the Contemporary* (Oxford, U.K.: Blackwell Publishers, 1997), 214.

6. Douglas Rushkoff, *The GenX Reader* (New York: Ballantine Books, 1994), 5.

7. Walter Truett Anderson, *Reality Isn't What It Used to Be* (San Francisco: Harper Collins, 1990), 37.

8. Anthropologists went into the field as neutral observers who refused to impose any of their own judgments on the cultures they studied. In so doing they avoided evaluating these cultures by our standards rather than those of the culture being studied and thus tainting their findings. They considered "primitive cultures" a good source of information regarding the basic building blocks of a culture. What they discovered was a wide range of beliefs, values, and customs.

    Upon returning home, anthropologists proclaimed the relativity of truth, that there are no absolute values, but that mores differ from culture to culture. The mores of our culture appear to be objective and absolute only because they are ours. Once exposed to the great diversity of human cultures, people were deeply affected. "Those who really took it in, in all its awesome variety, experienced a deep psychological disturbance that has sometimes been described as the 'vertigo of relativity,'" writes Walter T. Anderson in *Reality Isn't What It Used to Be* (Harper Collins, 1990). "They saw overwhelming evidence that different peoples had constructed entirely different systems of value and belief, knowledge and myth." Once it became apparent that other peoples had "invented" their cultures, the light was then trained on the culture of the researchers and revealed it to be a human invention as well. When performing field research in other cultures, Anderson says, "the anthropologist discovers that he or she is also living in a culture, not simply in objective reality" (p. 38).

9. Friedrich Nietzsche, *The Will to Power,* trans. Walter Kaufmann and R. J. Hollingdale (New York: Vintage Books, 1968), 291.

10. For Jean Baudrillard, Disneyland is a good example of hyperreality, a fabricated environment of interconnecting signs and symbols that replaces reality. But one does not exit hyperreality when leaving Disneyland, for the theme park merely masks the truth about the world outside: "Disneyland is presented as imaginary in order to make us believe that the rest is real, whereas all of Los Angeles and the America that surrounds it are no longer real, but belong to the hyperreal order and to the order of simulation. It is no longer a question of a false representation of reality (ideology) but of concealing the fact that the real is no longer real, and thus of saving the reality principle" (See *Simulacra and Simulation,* Ann Arbor: University of Michigan Press, 1999, pp. 12-3).

The "real" world has been blanketed by hyperreality, which descends over the landscape like a huge map covering everything underneath, so the landscape is lost and the map is all one sees. We travel this unreal space, following signs that point to other signs, on our hyperreal freeways that crisscross and return to themselves in spaghetti-like fashion.

The movie *The Matrix* is an excellent example of seeing through the hyperreality of our everyday world. It challenges our notions of what is real, causing us to wonder if we would be able to tell the difference between the real world and a digitized world made to seem real in every way. In the beginning of the movie, Neo has hidden some bootlegged computer disks in a hollowed-out book. The camera captures the title of the book—Baudrillard's *Simulacra and Simulation.* But this is not the bright, glossy paper cover you are likely to find if you come across his book in a bookstore. No, this is an old-looking, leather-bound book, as if it has already been around for a long time, its contents taken for granted. It could almost look like a Bible, and perhaps that is the intention; Baudrillard has written the bible for finding one's way around in this new, virtual universe.

11. Edward Veith, *Postmodern Times: A Christian Guide to Contemporary Thought and Culture* (Wheaton, Ill.: Crossway, 1994), 124,127.

12. Ian Mitroff and Warren Bennis, *The Unreality Industry: The Deliberate Manufacturing of Falsehood and What It Is Doing to Our Lives* (New York: Oxford University Press, 1993), xxii,55.

13. Postmodern filmmakers explore the fuzzy edges of reality in a variety of ways. For example, *This Is Spinal Tap* is a documentary-type film that takes viewers on a concert tour with a rock-'n'-roll band. When the band is playing live (which is certainly a confusing term when referring to prerecorded events), we the viewers are taken onstage and backstage. We follow band members into dressing rooms and move among the wild crowds. We see interviews with the members as they philosophize about life and share their feelings about being a rock star. We also witness their lives on the road.

But *This Is Spinal Tap* is a parody, not a documentary. There was no Spinal Tap band at the time, although one was formed later as a result of the movie. Nevertheless, the format of the movie is so deceiving many people who saw it thought they were watching a genuine documentary.

What the pseudodocumentary proves is that *all* rock bands are mere simulations, that there is a huge capitalistic industry that manufactures stars for the profit of the producers, record companies, and performers, and that the commercialism of rock music ensures that it will always exist within popular culture as a movement of breadth without depth.

Some postmodern screenwriters and moviemakers have experimented with "magical realism." Plots unfold in a seemingly normal setting, but they introduce fantasy elements that are treated as plausible. Edward Veith highlights the miraculous or magical elements in movies like *Groundhog Day*, *L. A. Story*, and *Field of Dreams*. These movies make no attempt to explain how the bizarre events that stand at the center of the plot ever could occur. "The fantastic premise is accepted at face value by the audience," says Veith, "and it is then worked out in ingenious detail."

Modern movies would not have been comfortable with this arrangement but would have provided some kind of rationale for paranormal occurrences. But such explaining is not necessary in postmodernity. "This is all magical realism. It is not conventional fantasy—no flights into other worlds, no medievalism, no ethereal dreaming. This fantasy is earthbound, grounded in a hard-edged, even depressing landscape in which wild, absurd, or wonderful things nevertheless take place" (*Postmodern Times*, pp. 132-3).

It is important to remember that television and movie cameras are extremely limited (they have no peripheral vision like human sight) and are therefore very selective in what they capture and transmit. Even greater selectivity goes into editing films and videos, and now there is the ever-present danger of computer-generated objects, characters, and events. We've all seen cartoon characters interacting with human beings.

14. Boris Vallejo, *Fantasy Art Techniques* (New York: Simon & Schuster, 1987), 14.

15. Anderson, *Reality Isn't What It Used to Be*, 5.

16. Heather Webb, "Hearing the Voice of the Other," *Mars Hill Review*, No. 12 (fall 1998): 21.

17. Mary Field Belenky, Blythe McVicker Clinchy, Nancy Rule Goldberger, and Jill Mattuck Tarule, *Women's Ways of Knowing: The Development of Self, Voice, and Mind* (New York: Basic Books, 1986), 115.

18. Leonard Sweet, *Quantum Spirituality: A Postmodern Apologetic* (Dayton, Ohio: Whaleprints, 1991), 265.

19. In exploring some of the ways postmodernity, in contrast to modernity, approaches the social sciences, Pauline Rosenau points out that learning for modern science required researchers to "isolate elements, specify relationships, and formulate a synthesis; post-modernists do the opposite." Postmodernists look for anomalies rather than constants, for "the unrepeatable rather than the re-occurring." She says, "Within a post-modern perspective social science becomes a more subjective and humble enterprise as truth gives way to tentativeness. Confidence in emotion replaces efforts at impartial observation. Relativism is preferred to objectivity, fragmentation to totalization" (*Post-Modernism and the Social Sciences,* Princeton, N.J.: Princeton University Press, 1992, p. 8).

Chapter 5

1. Donald Hustad, *Jubilate! Church Music in the Evangelical Tradition* (Carol Stream, Ill.: Hope Publishing, 1981) 227.

    I value Donald Hustad's insights and balanced treatment of church music. His preferences are obvious, but he is certainly much more gracious to contemporary Christian music than many of his colleagues.

    Every generation seems to bring its own innovation to worship, and this is especially true with the acceleration of cultural changes in the last one hundred years. Every youth culture has to deal with the church's gatekeepers (oftentimes elders or ushers) in order to bring their instruments (or musical style) through the doors of the sanctuary.

    Here is how Hustad sees it in *Jubilate!*: "It is interesting to note that each new form of youth entertainment music is greeted with the charge that it is conducive to immoral and anti-social behavior, but those fears are usually forgotten when the next style is introduced and the earlier becomes 'old hat.'

Only a few evangelicals are dogmatic enough to say that rock-gospel music was devil-inspired or even communist-oriented. In fact, many more have found some of the new forms to be effective media for communicating the gospel to today's young people" (p. 21).

Every church eventually comes under the domination of an old guard that resists the new wine of the current season. Members of the old guard prefer the old wine because they are convinced "the old is better" (Luke 5:39). These devotees to local traditions often expend their resources and energy trying to recapture (or preserve) something wonderful that happened many years ago. They find it hard to believe that God cuts new channels for the sake of reaching new generations. On the other hand, the youth find it nearly impossible to make the old forms of worship truly their own and to express their faith as passionately as they do with their own cultural forms.

2. For example, the first time a preacher equated women's slacks with the Deuteronomy passage about clothing "which pertaineth to a man," he was correct. But Deuteronomy does not make an eternal statement about slacks, only about a sexual issue that we refer to as "cross-dressing"—men trying to mimic women and women trying to mimic men. In past eras, when "men wore the pants" in society, only a cross-dressing woman would dare to wear them.

But fashions change and sometimes redefine what is considered acceptable. When that happens, we need to review and revise our interpretation of the Scriptures so that the Bible continues to speak to the real issues of our lives in a relevant way. My heart's desire is to see a new response to popular culture from the church. Rather than give people the impression that God was for yesterday, I want to see Christians represent the truth: that the God who identified Himself as "I AM" is for today and tomorrow and forever. With the advent of postmodernity we have an opportunity to reenter public life as a force for good and with new vitality in our message. But this means we need to listen both to popular culture and to the Bible for fresh interpretations that will fit the times in which we live.

3. Allen Wheelis, *The End of the Modern Age* (New York: Harper & Row, 1971), 36.

4. Bill Bright, *Have You Heard of the Four Spiritual Laws?* (Orlando: Campus Crusade for Christ, 1965).

5. Wheelis, *The End of the Modern Age,* 43.

6. How often have you heard the phrase "Christ's finished work on the cross"? Ray Anderson, in *The Soul of Ministry* (Louisville, Ky.: Westminster John Knox, 1997), suggests that Jesus' work was not finished on the cross. If not for the resurrection, he argues, there would be no atonement.

He describes a theology class in which he brought this issue before his students. "I read from Paul's letter to the Corinthians, 'If Christ has not been raised, your faith is futile and you are still in your sins. Then those also who have died in Christ have perished' (1 Cor. 15:17-18). It is the resurrection of Jesus, not just his death on the cross, that completed the atonement, I went on to suggest. The reason for this is that it is not just sin that needs to be forgiven, but death that needs to be overcome. The consequence of sin is death.... And the great human dilemma is death, not merely sin" (p. 98). Therefore our belief in the resurrection of Jesus Christ is just as critical as our belief in His crucifixion. (See also Clark Pinnock, *Flame of Love: A Theology of the Holy Spirit,* Downers Grove, Ill.: InterVarsity, 1996, p. 99.)

7. Dietrich Bonhoeffer, *The Cost of Discipleship* (New York: Macmillan, 1963), 45-86.

. The English word *symbol* is derived from the Greek word *symbolon* (*syn-* means "with" or "together," *ballein* means "to throw"). A symbol consists of two things thrown together because of some obvious or implied relationship between them. So a dove with an olive branch in its beak is a symbol of peace and the cross a symbol of Christianity.

As far as symbols being avenues to faith, we should remember that this was the method Jesus employed with His parables. The same Greek root word appears in the term *parable* (*ballein* and *para-,* "with" or "alongside"), so in a parable, two things are thrown alongside each other (i.e., a seed can symbolize the teaching of Jesus in Matthew 13:1-23). Jesus used stories of ordinary events, objects, and relationships to illustrate the spiritual kingdom of God. Symbols illumine truth and guide us to faith.

9. Eugene Peterson, *The Contemplative Pastor: Returning to the Art of Spiritual Direction* (Grand Rapids: Eerdmans, 1994), 32-3.

10. Walter Brueggeman, *Cadences of Home: Preaching Among Exiles* (Louisville, Ky.: Westminster John Knox Press, 1997), 32,59.

Since there is a danger that listening to symbols through our imagination may result in a distortion of the truth, Anthony Thiselton, in *Interpreting God and the Postmodern Self* (Grand Rapids: Eerdmans, 1995), further explains Paul Ricoeur's suggestion that "we work with a 'hermeneutic of suspicion' alongside a more constructive 'hermeneutic of retrieval.' Hermeneutics may be summed up in the two principles: 'willingness to suspect,' which destroys idols, and 'willingness to listen,' which retrieves the power of symbols and communicative texts" (p. 69).

11. At times, premodern thinking has been characterized as "naive realism," the belief that reality as we perceive it is identical to reality "out there." Premoderns did not concern themselves with the distance between the real world and language. Postmodern writers, on the other hand, make a big deal over the distinction between signifiers (symbols such as words or signs) and the signified (what those symbols represent)

Postmoderns borrow from linguists (or more properly, semioticians) the understanding that there is no natural reason why a word, such as *car*, should evoke in our minds a specific object (a transportation vehicle for passengers, with wheels, powered by an electric or combustion engine). The connection between words and objects is arbitrary, a social convention or code that enables two people to communicate. Language, in postmodernity, is disconnected from reality.

Premodern folks might find truth or reality within a story, but if postmoderns find reality, it exists alongside the story. In premodernity, if the storyteller was credible, then the message was most likely true. Not much analysis was required by the hearers; they could simply decide whether they believed the storyteller or not. In postmodernity we have a different situation and a different kind of challenge.

If language is discrete from the "real world," then stories have a different significance today than in premodernity. The people who sit in our churches at Christmas and Easter—and listen to the stories of Jesus' birth, death, and resurrection—have a different way of relating to our stories than those of us who believe not only in their symbolic meaning but also their literalness.

It is tempting to think of fundamentalist Christianity as premodern because of its tendency to simplify to the extreme. Some fundamentalists believe they can win arguments, resolve conflicts, dissolve doubt, and present a powerful defense of Christianity merely by saying, "The Bible said it, I believe it, and that settles it." These people preserve the simplicity of premodernity, but their arguments have all the weight of helium in postmodern discourse.

12. One of the first and most important voices in modern (liberal) theology was Friedrich Schleiermacher, whose massive work *The Christian Faith* was an intellectual and innovative challenge to old systems of interpretation. Echoes of Schleiermacher still ring in almost all of Protestant theology. His theology

was modernized in the sense that it fully embraced the tenets and beliefs of the Enlightenment.

According to Stanley Grenz, "To traditionalists [Schleiermacher's] *The Christian Faith* represented a capitulation to the antisupernaturalist spirit of the Enlightenment age, a thinly disguised attempt to talk about humanity as if it were talk about God. To progressives it represented a liberation from outmoded authoritarian dogmatics and to a truly modern form of Christian faith that would not conflict with science. Its publication unleashed a hurricane of harsh criticism with charges of pantheism and the like. It also loosened a flood of revisionist theologies seeking to follow in Schleiermacher's footsteps and refashion Christianity to appeal to modern secular audiences" (Stanley Grenz and Roger Olson, *Twentieth Century Theology*, Downers Grove, Ill.: InterVarsity, 1992, p. 42).

13. George Marsden, *Understanding Fundamentalism and Evangelicalism* (Grand Rapids: Eerdmans, 1994), 118-19.

14. Scott Peck's *The Different Drum* (New York: Simon & Schuster, 1987, pp. 187-200) presents a helpful model of "The Stages of Spiritual Growth." It's useful in conceptualizing the progress Christians make through their first years of faith, then into the hard years when the "romance wears off" and the trials intensify, eventually leading to the more peaceful years of spiritual maturity.

Peck identifies four stages. The first, which isn't really anything because there is no spiritual life, he calls "chaotic, antisocial." Stage two he calls "formal, institutional." Stage three is "skeptic, individual," and the fourth stage is "mystic, communal." The last three stages are remarkably similar to the responses I have identified in John 20 as "simple," "skeptical," and "symbolic" and to premodern, modern, and postmodern faith.

Premodern faith correlates to Peck's stage two, formal and institutional. It is formal because one characteristic of people in this stage is "their attachment to the forms (as opposed to the essence) of their religion." It is institutional because people develop a dependency on the institution of the church to keep them living right. When Christians remain in the comfortable world of this stage, where every decision is rendered in black-and-white terms, they tend to become legalistic in their attitude toward themselves and others.

Peck's third stage of spiritual growth is a time of questioning and doubting—the Thomas stage. People in this stage have discovered that the simple formulas one often learns as a new Christian do not work. They wonder why the Christians who have a strong investment in holding forth the truth are so lacking in love. They wonder if everything they have been taught is true or fair to people of other faiths. They are drawn to the gray areas of Christian ethics and theology. This stage can be frightening to enter (at first you feel as if you are losing your religion) and terrifying for people stuck in stage two to watch their companions enter. (Fundamentalists in stage two often fear their friends moving into stage three are becoming liberals.)

Stage four of Peck's model correlates to postmodern faith, the symbolic response of believers who do not need to see in order to believe. These people love mystery. Though they labored long and hard over the seeming contradictions and tough problems of their faith in stage three, they no longer need all the answers. They are content with the ambiguities that always are present in authentic spirituality. Peck makes an important point regarding the attitude that people have toward others who are further along in these stages of growth. He writes: "Perhaps predictably, there exists a sense of threat among people in the different stages of religious development. Mostly we are threatened by people in the stages above us.... Stage II people are not threatened by Stage I people, the 'sinners.' They are commanded to love sinners. But they are very threatened by the individualists and skeptics of Stage III, and even more by the mystics of Stage IV, who seem to believe in the same sorts of things they do but believe in them with a freedom they find absolutely terrifying. Stage III people, on the other hand, are neither threatened by Stage I people nor by Stage II people (whom they simply regard as superstitious) but are cowed by Stage IV people, who seem to be scientific-minded like themselves and know how to write good footnotes, yet somehow still believe in this crazy God business" (pp. 194-5).

15. Simone Weil, "Attention and Will," *Simone Weil: An Anthology*, ed. Sian Miles (New York: Weidenfeld & Nicolson, 1986), 215.

16. Esther De Waal, *The Celtic Way of Prayer: The Recovery of the Religious Imagination* (New York: Doubleday, 1997), 38-40,47-8.

17. Bright, *Have You Heard of the Four Spiritual Laws?*

18. Diogenes Allen, *Christian Belief in a Postmodern World: The Full Wealth of Conviction* (Louisville, Ky.: Westminster John Knox Press, 1989), 7.

19. Allen, *Christian Belief in a Postmodern World*, 7.

20. Sweet, *Quantum Spirituality*, 235.

21. Walter Truett Anderson, *Reality Isn't What It Used to Be* (San Francisco: Harper Collins, 1990), 187.

22. Allen, *Christian Belief in a Postmodern World*, 8.

23. Ted Peters, *God—The World's Future: Systematic Theology for a Postmodern Era* (Minneapolis: Fortress Press, 1992), 19.

24. Peters, *God—The World's Future*, 19-20.

25. Charles Tart, *States of Consciousness* (New York: E. P. Dutton, 1975), 38.

26. Walter Truett Anderson, *The Truth About the Truth: De-confusing and Reconstructing the Postmodern World* (New York: Tarcher/Putnam, 1995), 69-70.

27. Peters, *God—The World's Future*, 43.

Chapter 6

1. Simon Chan, *Spiritual Theology: A Systematic Study of the Christian Life* (Downers Grove, Ill.: InterVarsity, 1998), 103.

2. Walter Brueggeman, *Cadences of Home: Preaching Among Exiles* (Louisville, Ky.: Westminster John Knox Press, 1997), 42.

3. Ray Anderson, *The Soul of Ministry* (Louisville, Ky.: Westminster John Knox Press, 1997), 183.

4. Ihab Habib Hassan, *The Dismemberment of Orpheus: Toward a Postmodern Literature* (New York: Oxford University Press, 1982), 267-268.

5. Paul Waitman Hoon, *The Integrity of Worship: Ecumenical and Pastoral Studies in Liturgical Theology* (Nashville: Abingdon, 1978), 153,184.

6. Russel Spittler, ed., *Perspectives on the New Pentecostalism* (Grand Rapids: Baker, 1976), 184.

7. Zygmunt Bauman, "The Self in a Consumer Society," *Echoes* (winter 1998): 27. Published by the Post-Modernity Project (renamed the Institute for Advanced Studies in Culture), University of Virginia. http://www.virginia.edu/iasc

8. Brueggeman, *Cadences of Home,* 35.

9. See Patricia Joplin's essay, "Intolerable Language: Jesus and the Woman Taken in Adultery," in *Shadow of Spirit: Postmodernism and Religion* (New York: Routledge, 1992), 226-37.

10. Leonard Sweet, *Quantum Spirituality: A Postmodern Apologetic* (Dayton, Ohio: Whaleprints, 1991), 29.

11. Evelyn Underhill, *Worship* (New York: Crossroad Publishing, 1982), 29,31.

Chapter 7

1. Lyle Schaller, *Understanding Tomorrow* (Nashville: Abingdon, 1978), 32-7.

2. My kids still use X as a symbol for a kiss. "Generation Kiss"? When I heard Leonard Sweet speak at a Postmodern/Gen X conference, he used the metaphor of a kiss to suggest one way Christians could influence their world. He said something to the effect: "The modern world began with a 95-point sermon, and ever since we've been making points." (He made a good point.) The liturgical kiss, he said, was a sacramental sign of love. He said that we touch Jesus through the sacraments and that we are to be touching others in the world as well. For Christians wanting to make inroads into postmodern popular culture, "X marks the spot."

3. See Bill Strauss and Neil Howe, *Generations: The History of America's Future, 1584 to 2069* (New York: William Morrow, 1991), 324-8 and also Bill Strauss and Neil Howe, *13th Gen: Abort, Retry, Ignore, Fail?* (New York: Vintage Books, 1993), 16,60,63.

4. Douglas Rushkoff, *The GenX Reader* (New York: Ballantine Books, 1994), 293.

5. Rushkoff, *The GenX Reader*, 294.

6. Strauss and Howe, *13th Gen*, 85.

7. Barbara Hargrove and Stephen Jones, *Reaching Youth Today: Heirs to the Whirlwind* (Valley Forge, Pa.: Judson Press, 1983), 23.

8. Cornel Bonca, "Punk Junkies: How to be part of the Zeitgeist without being onto it," *OC Weekly*, 12-18 November 1999, 36.

9. Graeme Codrington, *Generation X: Who, What, Why and Where To?* 1998, 8. Internet site: http://home.pix.za/gc/gc12/genx/thesis

10. Tom Beaudoin, *Virtual Faith: The Irreverent Spiritual Quest of Generation X* (San Francisco: Jossey-Bass Publishers, 1998), 47.

11. Beaudoin, *Virtual Faith,* 41-2. I would recommend this book to anyone hoping to have a spiritual influence on this generation. Beaudoin discerns four religious themes in popular culture. First, there is a "deep suspicion of religious institutions." This is evident in the current spate of movies that contain antichurch (especially anti-Roman Catholic Church) plots. Second, popular culture emphasizes "the sacred nature of experience. Lived experience becomes a key indicator of what counts as religious." Third, there is the "religious dimension of suffering," especially the "varieties of suffering that the generation has endured." Fourth, popular culture is engaged in "an exploration of faith and ambiguity."

12. If you don't think Gen X (and Y) live in a different world from ours, consider the following: Every year the staff at Beloit College in Wisconsin creates a list of factors in the lives of their incoming freshmen in order to better understand their mind-set. Here are a few items from their 1999 list:
    - The people who are starting college this fall across the nation were born in 1980.
    - They have no meaningful recollection of the Reagan Era and did not know he had ever been shot.
    - They were prepubescent when the Persian Gulf War was waged.
    - Black Monday 1987 is as significant to them as the Great Depression.
    - There has been only one pope. They can only really remember one president.
    - They were eleven when the Soviet Union broke apart and do not remember the Cold War.
    - They have never feared a nuclear war.
    - They are too young to remember the space shuttle blowing up.
    - Tiananmen Square means nothing to them.

- Their lifetime has always included AIDS.
- Bottle caps have always been screw off and plastic.
- Atari predates them, as do vinyl albums.
- The expression "You sound like a broken record" means nothing to them.
- They have never owned a record player. Of course, they are aware of vinyl albums and turntables if they listen to rap music. But that is putting the record player to a very different use than just listening to music.
- They have never played Pac Man and have never heard of Pong.
- *Star Wars* looks very fake to them, and the special effects are pathetic.
- The compact disc was introduced when they were a year old.
- Most have never seen a television set with only thirteen channels, nor have they seen black-and-white television.
- There have always been VCRs, but they have no idea what BETA is.
- *The Tonight Show* has always been with Jay Leno.
- Popcorn has always been cooked in the microwave.
- Kareem Abdul-Jabbar is a football player.
- The Vietnam War is as much ancient history to them as WW I, WW II, or even the Civil War.
- They have no idea that Americans were ever held hostage in Iran.
- They never heard "Where's the beef?" "I'd walk a mile for a camel" or "De plane, boss, de plane!"
- Kansas, Chicago, Boston, America, and Alabama are places, not music groups.

13. Douglas Rushkoff, *Playing the Future: What We Can Learn from Digital Kids* (New York: Riverhead Books, 1999), 23.

14. For further reading on the Gen X sense of entitlement, look at Peter Sacks's book *Generation X Goes to College* (Chicago: Open Court Publishing, 1998).

Sacks explains how he first tried his hand at teaching in a local college. He went into the classroom with the assumption that education in the nineties was the same as when he was in college. Because of poor student evaluations, he came close to not qualifying for tenure. He determined that most of his Gen X students expected a lot of handholding, spoon-feeding, and entertainment from their professors. When he experimented with some advice he was given to "teach to the evaluations," as if they could only learn through a Sesame Street format, his student evaluations improved, and he was granted tenure.

Though his assessment of Gen X could have been better researched and his cynicism tends to cloud important issues, such as the real brilliance of this generation (which may never show on SAT scores), his book is worth reading just to demonstrate the frustration many boomers feel toward what they see as the "slacker generation." His conclusions in chapter 14, "Adapting to a Postmodern World," offer a few useful suggestions regarding the education of Gen X.

15. Rushkoff, *Playing the Future*, 4.

16. Hargrove and Jones, *Reaching Youth Today*, 55

17. The more rigid religious people of my growing-up years were certain they knew what the church "ought" to be. It should be dedicated to education rather than entertainment; it should be a place of reverence rather than fun; people should repress their personal problems to maintain a saintly image. They also were convinced that young people should stick to tradition and not attempt to innovate rituals, liturgy, or Bible study.

18. If the church does not explore new structures for Gen X believers, we have a lot to lose. For example, we will miss an important opportunity to revitalize our churches with youth. Young people are the church's future. Second, we will miss an opportunity to set up beachheads in popular culture and estab-

lish a Christian presence to a degree that was not possible in modernity. Third, we will require the culture-conversion of Xers who do join our churches, and that will damage them emotionally and spiritually. The church has a sad, unfortunate history of requiring more of new converts than what God requires (see Acts 15).

There is a price to pay for being out of step with one's culture. True, Christians are different from non-Christians, but many believers fail to see that the difference is primarily a *spiritual* difference, and if we constantly stress external differences, we have degenerated from grace into legalism. But this is exactly the kind of Christianity under which young people often are yoked by their leaders (Acts 15:10). They are buried under a truckload of duties intended to effectively remove them from any engagement with popular culture.

Outside of popular culture, Christians are encouraged to gather in a religious subculture that has as little to do with the "world" as possible. According to Mansell Pattison in *Religious Movements in Contemporary America* (Princeton, N.J.: Princeton University Press, 1974, p. 444), "Fundamentalists form a functional discrete subculture and remain marginal members of society. For them an ideal society exists for the members, a 'sacred society' experienced through church-related interests and activities." We forget that God had only anger for the people who said, "Stand by thyself, come not near to me; for I am holier than thou" (Isaiah 65:5, KJV). The *apparent* reason we want non-Christians to keep their distance is because we are afraid of being defiled. Perhaps the real reason is that we fear once we get close enough to know each other, we will discover we are more alike than different.

19. Codrington, *Generation X*, 8.

20. Strauss and Howe, *Generations: The History of America's Future*, 43, 218.

21. Lyle Schaller, *Understanding Tomorrow* (Nashville: Abingdon, 1978), 28.

Chapter 8

1. John Stott, *Between Two Worlds: The Art of Preaching in the Twentieth Century* (Grand Rapids: Eerdmans, 1982), 138,140.

2. There is another benefit to speaking in the language of popular culture and addressing its issues: Our communication becomes more interesting and more useful to those of us who are already believers! There are Christians who are afraid that if the church focuses on contemporary issues, mature believers will not receive the meat of God's Word. But the truth is, if we constantly learn how to live our Christian faith in the real world, then we will do a better job of being the kind of believers who influence others in a positive way. We will be light and salt. The problem with a lot of biblical teaching is that it locates our information in history but fails to help us connect that information with today's world.

3. For the last thirty years at least, it has been popular for Bible teachers to talk about the "propositional truths" of the Bible. This is a typically modern phenomenon: Dissect (exegete) the Bible in a scientific manner (biblical criticism), and it will yield "propositions." But closely examining the Scriptures in search of propositional truths may throw us off the trail of what God intends to do in our lives through His Word. Maybe God did not mean for us to walk away from our study of Scripture armed with propositions. Rather, God's intent is that we have a life-transforming encounter with Jesus Christ (John 5:39-40).

   Our search for propositional truths may obscure the fact that what lie before us are unavoidable commands. It is one thing to admire the brilliance and profundity of Scripture, but it is another thing to do what it says. One of the problems of looking for propositional truths is that we inevitably *use* the text of the Bible rather than *experience* it—as a hammer, fire, and sword that cuts to the bone (Jeremiah 23:29; Hebrews 4:12).

We can "use" the Scripture for our ends (e.g., to prove our particular doctrinal statement). But we need to find ourselves caught in the power of Scripture, rather than having that power at our fingertips. If we are *using* the Bible for our purposes, whether noble or otherwise, then it becomes no more than religious technology, a tool that increases our power. But when God's Word converges with His Spirit on our hearts and minds, then we are confronted by a power that is His alone and to which we must yield or be broken.

Clark Pinnock points out that though the quest for propositional truth has become the favorite method of evangelical Bible study, it is only one way to approach interpretation. In *Flame of Love* (Downers Grove, Ill.: InterVarsity, 1996, p. 220), he observes: "The evangelical emphasis on the propositional nature of truth has directed attention almost entirely toward biblical exegesis, to the neglect of other dynamics involved in interpretation. Those who like to call themselves biblical Christians often think of themselves as unaffected by the historical processes that affect others. We suffer from a naive realism, as if our interpretations have sprung without mediation from our reading of the Bible. We sometimes act as if historical elements played no part in them. It is not so."

4. Wesley Kort, *"Take, Read": Scripture, Textuality, and Cultural Practice* (University Park, Pa.: Pennsylvania State University Press, 1996), 129.

5. Kort, *"Take, Read,"* 128.

6. Clark Pinnock, *Flame of Love: A Theology of the Holy Spirit* (Downers Grove, Ill.: InterVarsity, 1996), 230.

7. Umberto Eco et. al., *Interpretation and Overinterpretation*, ed. Stefan Collini (New York: Cambridge University Press, 1992), 107.

8. Helmut Thielicke, *The Waiting Father* (New York: Harper & Row, 1975), 55.

9. Christians have not given enough thought or discussion to media churches or

televangelism, which are *all image*. There may be preaching, prayer, and singing over the radio, television, and Internet, but there is no *incarnation*, no point at which the Word becomes flesh, no physical contact with other living people. Televangelists may work hard at creating the illusion of intimacy and community, but how can there be community when we are not personally caring for one another's needs, when we are not being cared for, and when the viewer's only participation is sending money?

Too much is lost in electronic communication. Body language and environment speak volumes more than mere words. Physical touch—the holy kiss—is a vital component of community. Community depends on the kind of relationship building that is impossible to enjoy with a media image. As Neil Postman pointed out in *Amusing Ourselves to Death* (New York: Penguin Books, 1986), television is incapable of creating "sacred space."

10. Several years ago I attended a forum for senior pastors from different parts of the country. Over dinner one evening I became acquainted with Randy Mayeux, who was working on a doctorate in communication. So I asked him, "What is the cutting edge of communication?" Without drawing a breath he said, "Narrative paradigm."

A few weeks later I received an essay from him that explained narrative paradigm, and it introduced me to a world of scholarship in communication and theology. Narrative paradigm is argumentation, persuasion, and the communication of facts through story. The story must have its own inner coherence and logic to be credible, but inside the story one is free from external constraints, yet the story can be convincing at the same time.

For example, when Aristotle analyzed communication in *Rhetoric,* he delineated three elements: *ethos* (the credibility of the speaker), *logos* (the underlying arguments and proofs), and *pathos* (arousing emotions and feelings in the audience). *Pathos* is the essence of narrative paradigm.

I wonder if we have passed through the phase of *ethos* in which every speaker was required to show his or her credentials, and *logos* in which the logical structure and facts were stressed, and now we are living in the age of *pathos*. The challenge today is to "show" people the truth.

11. Kathleen Norris, *Amazing Grace: A Vocabulary of Faith* (New York: Riverhead Books, 1998), 3.

About the Author

Chuck Smith, jr. came to faith in the chaotic milieu of the Jesus movement in the late sixties. Driven by the urgency of that apocalyptic era, he joined the hundreds of other young people traveling up and down the West Coast trying to convert as many people as possible. After teaching Bible studies in homes and on high school campuses for two years, he planted his first church in 29 Palms, California, when he was twenty years old. In 1975 he moved to Dana Point and began to refine his understanding of theology and biblical studies. He describes his life as "grace-filled" and is overwhelmed by all of the undeserved blessings he enjoys daily with his family and in his ministry.

author's meaning 3F

Descartes 205

postmodern god 206

Modern/Post-modern grounding 25

3 THINGS WE NEED TO KNOW 25